On Duty...

interviews with military veterans
from north of Quabbin

volume one

ON DUTY

by Alan W. Bowers

Haley's
Athol, Massachusetts

International Standard Book Number: 1-884540-09-0
International Standard Book Number (series): 1-884540-08-2
Library of Congress Catalogue Number: 94-78652
Library of Congress Catalogue Number (series): 94-78649 .

Copy read by Marcia Gagliardi and R. Rand Haven, Jr.
Proofs by Cotter Communications.
Image-making and printing by The Highland Press.
Text established in Microsoft Word 5.1a and 6.0.
Maps edited in Adobe Illustrator 5.5.
Layout and design formatted in Aldus Pagemaker 5.0.

Haley's
Post Office Box 248
Athol, Massachusetts   01331
508.249.9400

To Theresa and our family

Contents

Photographs

Maps

On Duty... Geography

Acknowledgments

I extend my appreciation, respect, and thanks to the veterans who granted me the privilege of recording their experiences: Gordon Briggs, Richard Chase, Leona Cloutier, Donald Corser, Armand Dugas, George Fiske, Peter Krustapentus, Earl Lindell, Henry Pierce, and Arthur Tarolli.

It is said the secret to success is to surround yourself with people who know their jobs and then be wise enough to get out of their way. Working with Marcia Gagliardi is the joy of watching a highly competent professional on task. With Rand Haven tending the copy, there is the certainty of attention to detail. I am very grateful to them.

The project is indebted to Mary Pat Spaulding for time and talents contributed as a consultant about design and illustrations, to John Cotter for proofs, and to Ted Chase for technical advice. I appreciate Dick Chaisson's encouragement, advice, and generosity with background materials. Debra Blanchard and Janice Lanou, directors at Athol Public Library and Wheeler Memorial Library, Orange, were unfailingly helpful in providing research material. I am grateful to everyone who has shared background information and materials.

How can I express enough appreciation to my bride of thirty-four years? Terri, you have experienced the whole gamut of a military career, from privilege to pain. At each step, you have shared the best and the worst, and you have always given your total support. From holding another late dinner to finding a treasure of research material in a flea market to juggling appointments and meetings, you have kept me on target. If there is a campaign ribbon for a spouse on duty above and beyond the call, you have certainly earned it.

Introduction

While there is no particular order or scheme involved in grouping veterans' memories, there is a common theme.

Each and every veteran answered the call to duty, did assigned tasks, and gave full talents whether drafted or enlisted, GI or officer, in the States or in a theater—and without regard to a particular branch of the service. Each and every veteran enjoyed the camaraderie of fellow servicemen and servicewomen and took pride in their contributions.

The following accounts are personal, often emphasizing interests of the individuals who shared them. In every case, it has been fascinating to realize how common and uncommon, unremarkable and unique, predictable and unanticipated the experiences of each individual have been.

Ideas and stories contained in this book are based on information from personal accounts provided by people interviewed. Therefore, the author and publisher accept responsibility only for accurately reporting the personal accounts. The author and publisher do not accept responsibility for the accuracy of information contained in these accounts. Nevertheless, attention has been given to corroboration of details in the personal accounts with common knowledge information available in general reference works. Readers should be advised that material in the following stories may be offensive to some people.

A Word From The Interviewer
What Is It About War Stories?

by Alan W. Bowers

Punching out of an OV10 observation aircraft—ejecting from the airplane when the right engine malfunctioned—led to quite a few changes in my life. That event on 17 September 1972 somewhere in the air over Southeast Asia between Thailand and Vietnam meant the end of a military career I had loved, thrived with, and cultivated for some fifteen years. At first, I couldn't imagine what I was supposed to do without it.

That powerful moment gave me the one thing none of us can buy—*time*. So, what should one do with such a precious commodity?

I opted for community service—especially veterans' services.

As I drove a member of the Charles Musante Chapter, Disabled American Veterans, to a Veterans Administration medical appointment, we talked about the thing we had most in common—our military experiences. His story enlightened and fascinated me. He agreed to let me tape record his memories, and he helped me fill in the blanks as I transcribed his story.

Sharing "war stories" has been a favorite pastime whenever veterans get together. Hearing some, I'd wonder if there weren't an occasional embellishment. After all, who doesn't like to top the other guy's story, and who doesn't want to be the best storyteller?

As I transcribed the tape recording about my friend's military career and wrote narration to provide necessary details in understandable gaps left by the enthusiasm of his story, I found my own memory triggering some experiences that might fall into the "top this" category. Even so, I asked others to let me tape record their stories of days in the military. I became convinced that there are important parts of military history being told *anywhere* that veterans get together. In this collection, to be published every six months over several years, I will tell my own story in greater detail, at an appropriate time.

So, then, I decided to seek out veterans and hear their stories. I decided to write down and share the interviews because I realize these interesting stories *must* be preserved.

In civilian life, veterans are ordinary people who go about their day-to-day business in the same way that you and I do. They are nobody special and everybody special, just as they were when they served Uncle Sam. There they were, putting their lives on the line, whether they were Stateside in peacetime or deep in combat during a war.

What sometimes becomes dry chapters in traditional history books was *real* to the men and women who served. Our friends and neighbors gave parts of their bodies and minds—and perhaps a nick of their souls—to do their duty. Their stories are the *real* history.

On the following pages—in no particular order and according to no particular scheme—are memories of our neighbors who answered their nation's call to duty.

On Duty...
Geography
volume one

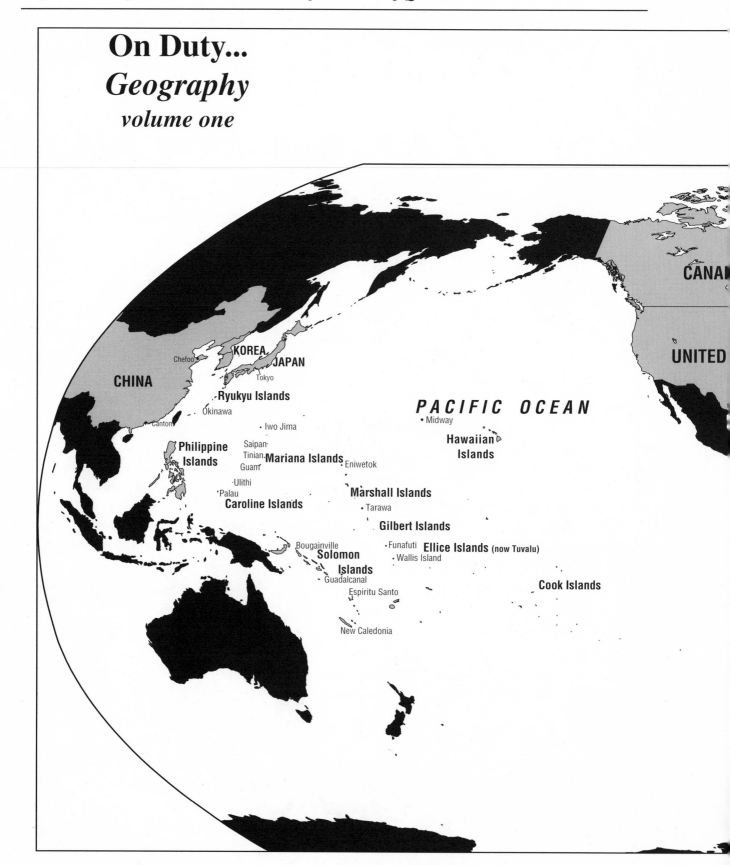

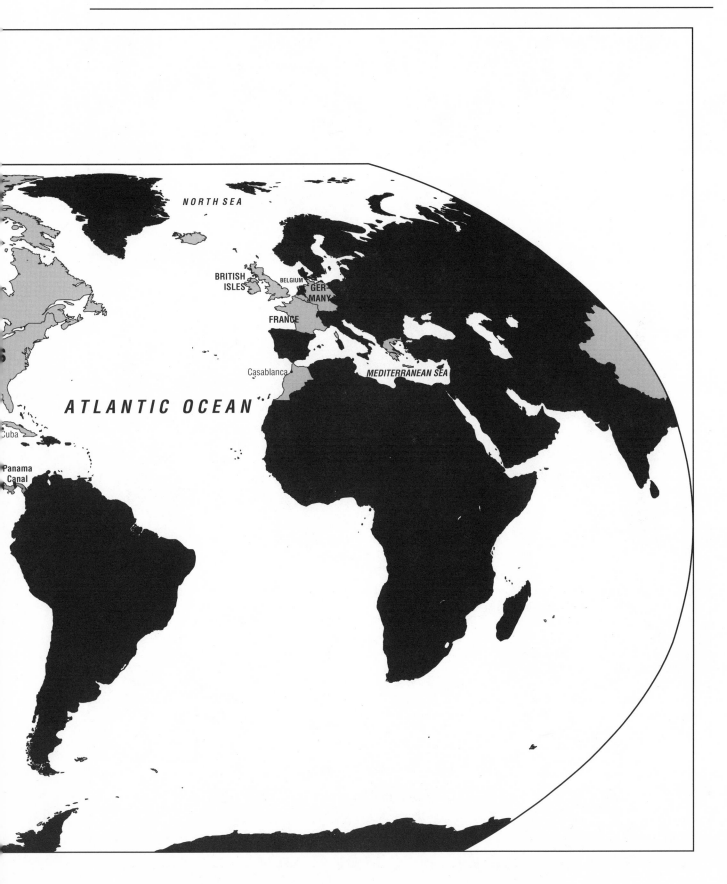

Earl "Lindy" Lindell Of Royalston   United States Navy, 1942-1961

Just Let Me Serve On A Submarine

Earl Lindell's first venture into military service was short-lived. Several of his friends joined the National Guard. Although under age, Earl also managed to sign up.

Twelve of us went in from Gilbert Stewart Junior High School in Rhode Island. When we got inducted, they sent us to Newport, Rhode Island, to Fort Adams. We got assigned to the 243rd Coast Artillery. We were a machine gun company. We went right in with the regular guys; no basic training. On 22 November 1941, we got a new commanding officer. He was our junior high principal. He discharged the twelve of us for being under age.

"Lindy" didn't have to wait long to realize his desire for military service. The country was soon at war, and by the next summer, he was old enough to join.

He had tried to jump the gun in 1941, but it wasn't too long before **EARL "LINDY" LINDELL**, then at home in Rhode Island, found himself wearing **"Navy blues."**

So when the war broke out, I went down to join the Marine Corps, to the Fargo Building in Boston. But when the guy made out my discharge for fraudulent enlistment from the National Guard, he listed my character as "good." The Marine sergeant told me they had orders from the commandant of the Marine Corps not to accept any ex-military personnel with character less than "excellent." That really shook me up. So I left his office and got into the elevator. There were three Navy captains in the elevator.

I showed the discharge to one of the captains and asked him if I could get into the Navy with that record. He pulled out a pad, wrote something on it, and sent me up to the sixth floor. I entered the Navy reserves on 25 March 1942.

That time Lindy got to experience basic training.

We were supposed to go to Newport for basic, but they had an outbreak of some fever, so they sent us to Great Lakes. While I was going

through basic training, it was six weeks because the war was on. I took up with this guy from Boston, K.O. Irish. He was the one who got me to volunteer for submarines. He thought if we volunteered for subs, we'd go back to New London to sub school. When we graduated, they gave us a twelve-hour liberty. I went ashore in Milwaukee, came back at midnight all "drunked up," and reported in for duty. The officer said "Don't report in, go get your sea bag and hammock. I've got orders for you." When I asked if it was New London, he said, "If it is, it's via San Francisco."

Eight submarine volunteers went by train to San Francisco. Their final destination would be Hawaii.

When we got to Treasure Island [in San Francisco Bay], they sent us over to Alameda, and from there, they flew us to Ford Island, Honolulu. We got there on a Sunday morning. There were about three thousand men milling around like cattle on the ball field. Here comes three jeeps to take us—there were twelve submariners by then—over to the sub base. They took us up to the squadron office, where you could look out and see all the boats tied up. I was looking out the window when the lieutenant said, "See anything you like, Son?"

I said, "That big one looks nice."

He said, "That's the *Nautilus*. Report to the tank tomorrow morning at seven o'clock with all your gear."

The "tank" was a one-hundred foot high water tower with stairs up the side and watertight locks at several levels where divers could enter. After a lock was flooded, a student entered the tower and escaped to the surface.

The next morning, I went to the training tank at seven o'clock and made two twelve-foot escapes and one twenty-five-foot escape. We used what

was called a Munson Lung, a flexible breathing bag tied to the chest. And we escaped up a line that had knots every so far. At each knot, we had to stop and take so many breaths so your lungs could contract. If you tried to hold your breath, the pressure would expand, and

> **The lieutenant said, "See anything you like, Son?"**
> **I said, "That big one looks nice."**
> **He said, "That's the *Nautilus*. Report to the tank tomorrow morning at seven o'clock with all your gear."**
> **....By nine o'clock, I was peeling spuds on the *Nautilus*.**

your lungs could rupture. There were instructors at various levels in the tank. By nine o'clock, I was peeling spuds on the *Nautilus*. We got under way at noon that same day.

The skipper, Captain William Brockman, was a graduate of the Naval Academy at Annapolis. He later became a bank president before getting activated. The USS *Nautilus* was 312 feet long and twenty-seven wide, with an operating depth of three hundred feet. An average crew was fifteen officers and eighty men.

He got us out on the dock, lined us all up, and said, "I see a lot of new faces on my crew. I want to get one thing straight. I'm not running a suicide galley. We will come back. But I will personally shoot the first son-of-a bitch that doesn't

fight."

Lindy described the conditions on board as "not too bad."

When we had more than sixty men on board, we had to go to "hot bunking." Each two bunks were assigned to three men. You worked four hours on and eight off. You got the bunk of the guy you woke up, and he got the bunk of the next guy he woke up.

Lindy had been designated a motor machinist mate, so he was assigned to the engine room. Diesels could be run only when the sub was on the surface, and that's when they charged the batteries. Each submarine was assigned a large section of the Pacific Ocean to patrol. On the fourth war patrol, conducted in the Solomons 13 December 1942 until 4 February 1943, Lindy's first run, the *Nautilus* crew earned a citation. The sub was ordered to Toep Harbor to rescue twenty-six adults and three children.

We were patrolling off Guadalcanal when we got orders to go into Bougainville on New Year's Eve to pick up French and American missionaries. There were twenty-one women and eight men. I guess three of them were children. While we had the nuns on board, we had orders not to engage in combat. The old man was really mad, because the whole Japanese fleet went right over us. He was looking out the

On Duty...
Geography
Lindy Lindell

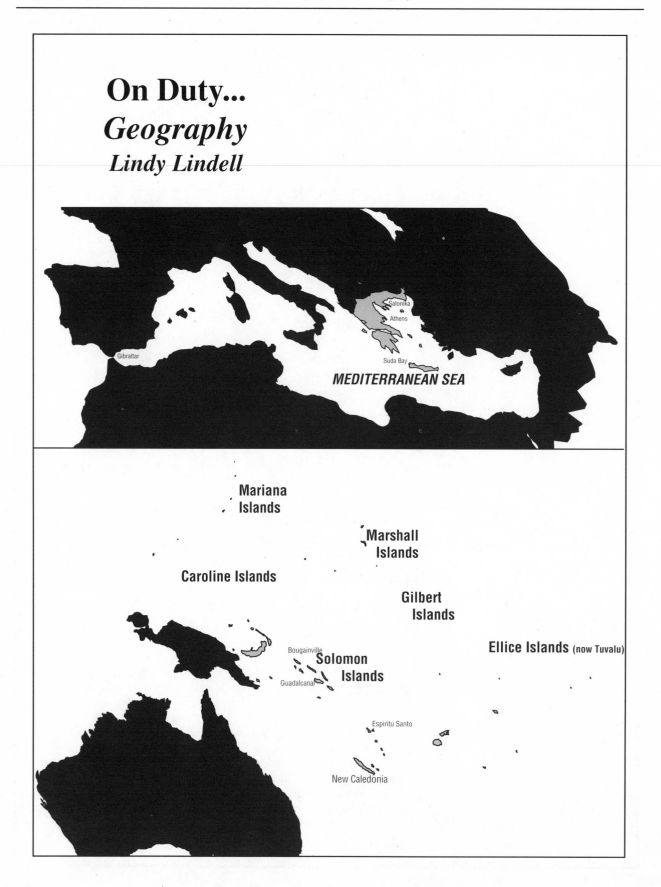

periscope, and he had tears running down his face.

We finally put the evacuees on an Australian cruiser. We wanted to take them to Australia, but we had another job to do. We were supposed to go up a river on Bougainville eight or nine miles to shell a radar station. There was only one catch. There wasn't enough water to turn around. We could have backed out, but it got canceled at the last minute.

History says *Nautilus (SS-168)* added the cargo ship *Yosinogawa Maru* to her kills and damaged a tanker, a freighter, and a destroyer before going to Mare Island near San Francisco, California, for overhaul. On 16 September 1943, the *Nautilus* slipped out of Pearl Harbor to start her sixth patrol in the Gilberts.

We carried Carlson's Raiders to Macon Island. We took Colonel Evan Carlson and Major James Roosevelt for the invasion. Roosevelt gave us coordinates over the radio, and we fired over the island and sank a gunboat. We had two six-inch guns, called "baggers" [the gunners inserted a projectile and two bags of powder]. When we submerged, we just opened the breech [so the water could flow through]. When we came up, we'd just blow the gun out and dry the breech.

Much of the sixth patrol involved conducting photo-reconnaissance, and it provided some of the most useful intelligence gathered in the Pacific. The *Nautilus* returned

to Pearl on 17 October 1943. By November, she was back at sea on patrol.

We got hit at Apamama, in the Gilberts. It was dark and foggy, and one of our destroyers picked us up on radar. I guess we didn't have a lot of faith in radar. On the *Nautilus,* the radar was run by the chief commissary steward. Sometimes, the Japs would home in on our radar, so we kept it turned off a lot.

At 2159 on 19 November, the American destroyer USS *Ringgold* mistook the *Nautilus* for an enemy sub and fired a five-inch shell.

It went through the conning tower. Fortunately, it was a dud. We returned to Pearl for repairs. When we tied up at Honolulu, the *Ringgold* tied up right behind us. The fur was flying for awhile.

On 4 December, the *Nautilus* again set out, this time for her eighth patrol, west of the Marianas. The records show the sub sunk one cargo ship and damaged three others.

When we took a shot at one of the Japanese ships, they'd come after us with depth charges. I can't explain how it felt, but once you've been through it, you never forget it. I can't remember how many times we went through that— more than I like to remember. I was sleeping in the after room where someone had partially unscrewed the light bulb. A depth charge went off, the light flashed, and I thought the whole

damned hull had ripped open. It gets nervous for a few minutes. We took some damage, but not much. They [the subs] were built good.

On later patrols, the *Nautilus* delivered ammunition, oil, and dry stores, landed reconnaissance parties, and patrolled around the Philippines. By January, 1945, she was routed home to Philadelphia. Before she departed, Lindy got assigned to the USS *Whale*, another submarine. The *Whale* had already had six war patrols; on her seventh, she sank the Japanese ship, *Honan Maru.*

I did four patrols on the *Whale* before the old man dumped me at Espiritu Santo, New Hebrides, just south of the equator. I had a little disagreement with the commissary officer, so he transferred me to a tender. I was on his shit list. They assigned me to the main engine room. With more time away from the States than anyone else, I was told I wouldn't be there very long. About midnight a few days later, a guy shook me. "Hey, Lindell, get your gear. There's a plane leaving and you're on it"

I flew back to Honolulu and then to Mare Island for thirty days' leave. I wanted a boat built there, but since I was from New England, they sent me back to New London. I took twenty-eight days of the thirty-day leave to get home. I travelled by train, but I made a lot of stops and even met some show girls headed for Milwaukee to put on some shows.

I was in the reserves so on 26 September 1945, I was sent to Electric Boat in Connecticut [the company building the new submarine] to put the *Halfbeak* into commission. I never got to put it into commission, because the war ended.

Out of the Navy, Lindy tried civilian life, including marriage, but that didn't work out. On 12 December 1947, he saw an opportunity to get back to submarines. He had been out more than 120 days, so he had lost his machinist mate rating.

The chief who was on recruiting duty in Boston had been with me during the war. He had been on the *Whale*. I went to see him about getting back in. He called me up about five o'clock that evening and said "Hey, Lindy, how about doing me a favor?"

I said, "What's up?"

He said, "My wife is sick, and I'm supposed to take the detachment to Bainbridge. Will you take them? They'll give you a set of orders to New London." Big and easy, I was back in the Navy.

We got to Bainbridge, and I was told to get in line. No one had told them I was prior service. They had me headed for boot camp. Then they found out I was prior service, so they put me in OGU [outgoing unit]. In the meantime, here comes a set of orders for me to go to Philadelphia to put a cruiser in commission. I wasn't too happy about that.

I went down to Philly. From there they sent us to Newport, Rhode Island, for fire fighting school. I'm raising hell, because I still wanted subs. So we went to school, and when we finished training and getting ready to go back to Philly, along comes a guy who says "Which one of you is Lindell?"

When I said "I am," he sent me up to the office. The chief warrant officer had been working on my request to go back to subs.

He said "Here you go. Here are your orders." They were to the Atlantic Submarine Command, headquartered in New London, Connecticut. That was a Friday. I got to New London about three o'clock in the afternoon and reported in to the squadron office. The chief said "What do you want for a boat?"

I said "What do you have?"

He showed me a new boat, the USS *Pomodon*, assigned to Panama.

I said "That's for me." So I returned Monday morning, looking for transportation to Panama. That's when I found out she was scheduled for eighteen months right there in New London. I went down to the end of the pier, and there she was. I was on her almost a year. Without the machinist mate rate, I worked as a fireman and as a mess cook. I had done duty with the chief mess cook during the war, so when he came back, I changed my rate from seaman to cook.

During that tour of duty, the boat was sent to Mare Island to become a *GUPPY* (Greater Underwater Propulsive Power Submarine). At Mare Island, some guns and clutter were removed. The conning tower was modified to make the sub more streamlined. A snorkel was added so the diesel could breathe while the sub was partially submerged. She was also assigned a trip to the Mediterranean. Next, Lindy was assigned to shore duty at Long Beach, California. While he was there, the Korean conflict broke out.

I was sent back to Mare Island to recommission the *Scabbard Fish* and right back out to Pearl. After a short tour on the *Scabbard Fish*, I transferred to the *K3*, a new type boat. They were a little smaller. She was also out of Honolulu.

During the Korean war, we just patrolled around Korea. There wasn't much Navy action. From the *K3*, I went to the *Tunny*—the funny *Tunny*. J. B. Osborn was the skipper [He was also the first skipper of the nuclear powered *George Washington*]. And, then, to shore duty at Key West.

My rate was frozen for promotions, so I decided to change my rate to ET [electronic technician]. That required a year's course at Great Lakes. I did six weeks of basic electronics, but I barely got by, so I wrote a letter requesting reassignment [back to subs]. The SOB left my rate off the reassignment, and I got assigned to an APA [amphibious assault], the USS *Chilton.* I wound up in the Med [Mediterranean].

Besides duty at sea, the USS *Chilton* had stops in Gibraltar, Athens, Suda Bay on the northern side of the island of Crete; France; Salonika in Greece, and Turkey. Early in the 1956 war between Israel and Egypt, the *Chilton* got orders to evacuate noncombatants from Alexandria, Egypt. The orders read in part, "...USE SHIP'S BOATS TO BRING OUT EVACUEES X LOCAL AUTHORITIES WILL HAVE ONE LAUNCH STANDING BY X IT APPEARS THAT BY TOMORROW MORNING THERE WILL BE 778 EVACUEES ..."

When the Jews first jumped on the Arabs, we went in and rescued the United Nations team.

Still wanting back into submarine duty, Lindy looked for every opportunity.

Later the Navy came out with a directive, "Any submarine personnel desiring reassignment to submarines should apply." We had an executive officer who had been a submarine officer. He had promoted me to E6, and he didn't want me to go.

We were coming into

Assigned to the diesel-powered USS *Barbel* at the beginning of the nuclear era, Lindy got an assignment that suited him. He preferred the diesels to the nuclear-powered.

Morehead City, Carolina. The yeoman called me up and said, "Lindy, we're sending two trucks up to Norfolk. Volunteer to drive one." He had a set of orders for me. I drove the truck to Norfolk and hauled ass for New London.

At New London, I wound up on the *Toro (SS-422)* doing school duty [training new submariners]. One of my students went down on the *Scorpion* and one on the *Thresher.* The Navy was pushing nukes [nuclear-powered submarines], and there was talk of the *Toro* going out of commission.

The old man told me I'd have to go nuke. I said, "No way." A couple of weeks later, he gave me a reprieve. They were building three new diesel boats, the *Bonefish, Barbel,* and *Blueback.*

The *Barbel* was being built at Portsmouth, New Hampshire. That was the same name as one of the subs sunk during World War II in the South Pacific while Lindy was serving there.

Always alert to opportunities in subs, Lindy almost met disaster. While still at Portsmouth, he retired with twenty-one and one-half years service.

The engineering officer of the *Thresher* guaranteed me E7 in ninety days if I signed on, but I already had my orders to retire on 20 February 1961.

Not long after the guarantee, the *Thresher* went down two hundred miles east of Boston. The date was 10 April 1963. In the Navy's worst peacetime submarine disaster, all 129 men were lost. Thanks to his retirement, Lindy wasn't one of them.

Henry Pierce Of Warwick   United States Navy Air Force, 1932 and 1941-1945

More Than 100 Missions—No Flight Rating

Henry Pierce's military career was predetermined by his boyhood adventure at Estey's Field in Orange, Massachusetts, "a dirt strip along the side of the road."

He started on a lark. He flew several hundred hours in a Piper *Cub*, but it cost too much, so he didn't keep it up. "Things were rough in 1928," he said, in reference to the pre-Depression economy he felt.

There's a *T*-shaped building along the side of Airport Road in Orange, Massachusetts, that looks like one of the original Estey's Field hangars. The upright of the *T* housed the tail and fuselage, and the crossbar of the *T* covered the wings.

Henry worked mostly as a woodcutter. He worked all over, anywhere someone would hire him. "I worked for the Great Northern Paper Company, up in Maine, cutting pulp, and picked potatoes in Caribou, Maine. Anywhere; it was tough." Henry enlisted in the Navy Air Force in 1928.

Basic training was at Newport, Rhode Island, for three months, and in Henry's words, "It was rough. Some of the barracks were from World War I."

You drilled from seven in the morning to five at night and sometimes afterward. We used to have to haul casings over the damned hills, which they don't do any more. Your uniform would be a mess by the time you came in, because you'd really sweat. We had to qualify

One of HENRY PIERCE's first assignments with the Navy Air Force was with *Old Ironsides***, the USS** *Constitution.*

with that old rifle, a pretty heavy job [probably the Enfield].

From Newport, his first assignment was to the USS *Constitution*, in 1930. He was in the fire department. His second assignment and first with a flying unit was to a lighter-than-air or dirigible unit in Cuba. His trip down to Cuba from Newport was aboard the USS *Reuben James*.

She was a hard luck ship; the one that "started the war." She was a four-stack oil burner.

On 31 October 1941, the USS *Reuben James* was sunk by a German submarine. It was the first warship lost by the United States Navy in the Battle of the Atlantic.

We hit a storm off Cape Hatteras. We didn't have any radar, any steering, except the after-station that was directly connected to the rudder. They couldn't steer it from the pilot's station. Everybody was sick. Boy, I'm telling you! Talk about stink!!

He never flew in his first assigned airship, the *Akron*. Built by Goodyear and christened on 8 August 1931 by Lou Henry Hoover, wife of President Herbert Hoover, the *Akron* crashed on 4 April 1933 off the coast of New Jersey near the Barnegat Lightship. Seventy-three men drowned.

The *Akron* went down at sea on its way to Cuba. The only

dirigible that made it to Cuba was the *Los Angeles*, a German gas job. It had been captured in WWI. U.S. blimps used helium.

Henry describes the "gas job" as some gas "that really

> **His first assigned airship, the *Akron*,...crashed off the coast of New Jersey near the Barnegat Lightship. Seventy-three men drowned. The *Akron* went down at sea on its way to Cuba.**

blew up."

Dirigibles were the most miserable things to moor; sometimes it would take six or seven hours to get one down. You had to discharge helium, sometimes practically half the helium on board. The ground crew had all the damned lines, then they had to dump a bunch of sandbags. Sometimes it took as many as twenty men to pull it down. I never saw it, but sometimes they even tied up on the Empire State Building in New York. I don't know how to hell they ever maneuvered them to get them moored. They had trouble getting the *Hindenburg* down at Lakehurst. It was dangerous work when the wind came up.

With no airship, he did temporary duty on a seagoing tug, the USS *Montcalm*, fixing buoys in the Caribbean. They would go around to the buoys by the islands with fuel for the lights. The *Montcalm* also took the garbage to dump at sea.

You should see the sea boil with fish when we dumped that garbage.

Henry finally got another assignment to a lighter-than-air unit in California. The USS *Dobbin*, a supply ship, provided the transportation through the Panama Canal.

It took us about three days to get through the Canal.

Docking at Sunnyvale, California, he was assigned to the USS *Utah*. The USS *Utah* "meal check" ticket in Henry's collection of memorabilia is evidence of that next temporary assignment.

The *Utah* was a hard luck bastard—one of the first to go down at Pearl Harbor.

Sunnyvale was not memorable, "just regular duty," although he never did fly in a lighter-than-air craft.

In 1932, his first hitch was up, and he returned to Warwick, Massachusetts. Flying was not in the cards. "Too damned expensive, and I didn't have the money." His mother lived in Rhode Island, so he worked cutting wood there for awhile. Then, he went back to the Warwick area cutting lumber. He bought an old truck to haul lumber, but "didn't make hardly anything. Old Sid Mann would come right into the woods, suit and all. He'd

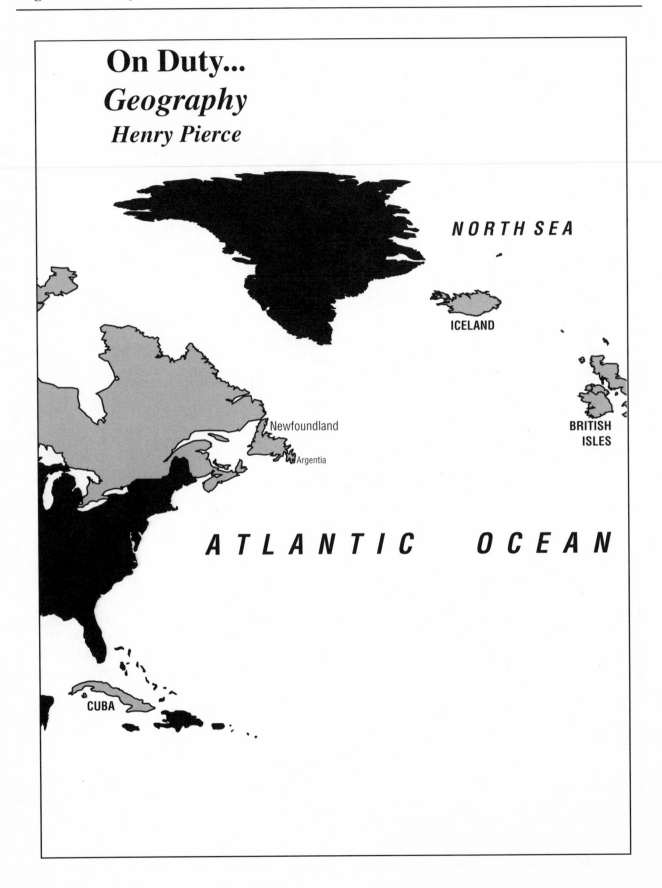

On Duty...
Geography
Henry Pierce

For a while, Henry was assigned to the USS *Utah*, "a hard-luck bastard," one of the first to go down at Pearl Harbor. Henry wasn't aboard then.

pitch right in. We set up the sawmill right in the woods." About 1940, Henry went into the L. S. Starrett Company, the precision toolmaker in Athol. Working at Starrett as a toolmaker, he heard about the attack on Pearl Harbor. A lot of men from Starretts' went into the service, and Henry went back to the Navy Air Force.

They sent me to Boston. "You are hereby authorized to return to 200 Milk Street for re-examination to be reassigned in the service. If you pass the examination, you'll be reassigned, and if not, your transportation will be paid back home." That's what they told me in the letter they sent.

I went down. They looked at my teeth, and I was in. Not much of a physical. Then we went over to the Fargo barracks. That was all old enlisted men who had retired and stuff like that. I was over there and then went down to Squantum Air Base [Squantum Naval Air

Station, near Quincy, Massachusetts] for two days of flight tests and two days of oral tests. The seventh day, it came over the speaker at midnight that we were to leave at seven the next morning. Our instructions were: "Your plane is over on Logan Air Base [the Army and Navy used it for military aircraft], and your orders are in the plane." We got over there—destination Argentia, Newfoundland. It was an old Lockheed *Lodestar*. They had knocked the bottom out and put in a bomb bay. They were trying to use it to bomb submarines, but that didn't work out. We went to New-foundland on that airplane as passengers.

In Argentia, they found a bunch of small two-engine British bombers. Each took a four man crew, two pilots and two gunners. They were dangerous because the gas tank was right behind the pilot. The loading gate was in the left oleo strut, and they were hot.

We ripped up most of them [the British airplanes]. Our run-

way was short, and when we couldn't stop them, we pulled up the gear. We didn't care about going in the drink. That tore up a lot of airplanes.

The military had a logistic structure, the ferry command, whose primary job was to deliver aircraft from the factory to the command area.

Then the ferry command dumped the B-24s [*Liberator* bombers built by Consolidated, with Pratt and Whitney engines] on the field. We had never seen one or even heard of them.

When asked if they had any instructions for this "never-seen" aircraft, Henry responded strongly, "Nope. Nothing."

We bounce-hopped them for about a week. The whole crew was *AEP*, all enlisted personnel. Practically all the *AEPs* were classified as machinist mates. When we went over, we had no spare parts. If you got a nick in a propeller, you filed a nick in the other propellers to keep them in balance. We had no brass. The brass didn't show up until we were there eight months.

As an enlisted flight captain, Henry was issued a .38-caliber handgun. "We didn't need rifles," he said.

All plane captains had .38s or .45s. The .45 was very inaccurate. You couldn't hit anything. The duty from Newfy was sub patrol from Newfoundland to Iceland and Greenland.

We sunk a couple [of subs], bombing them with "five-hundred-pounders" [five-hundred-pound depth charges]. We carried about five thousand rounds of ammunition. We had one submarine that put a hole right up through the wing. We got that airplane back okay, and no one was hurt. We landed at Reykjavik, Iceland. Later, we sunk a German sub right at the nets. An awful lot of ships were sunk in the North Atlantic.

Two hills bordered the front of a bay protected by a net stretched across it to keep out enemy subs. The hills were referred to as "Mae West" by the Navy men there. The harbor was home for United States Navy subs and PBYs, or seaplanes.

After eleven months on sub patrol from Newfy, we were told we were going to get orders. Since some of the gun turrets had been removed to cut out weight, we had from midnight to seven o'clock the next morning to put them all back [Guns were not needed for an-tiaircraft defense since there were no enemy airplanes around Newfy]. We were happy. We thought we were going back to the States. Then the orders came in—to Bristol, England.

Henry was the copilot in B-24s, and his regular duty was sub patrol.

We worked over the English channel and that's where we took most of our losses. Our B-24s were mostly shot down by JU-88s, a top of the line German fighter. Of the fifteen hundred men that went over together, only eighty-three came home.

Our crew got shot up twice. One time, we had to come in on our belly; it was mostly damage to the landing gear. We got jumped by a flock of JU-88s. I can't tell how many, but the B-24 had such firepower, if there were only three or four, they would stay their distance. I can't say if we shot any of them down. Nothing was recognized as shot down unless it was on a gun camera. No one was seriously hurt on that attack.

We made it back to Dunswell. That was one of the highest fields in England, and sometimes you'd get up the next morning and find airplanes nose to tail. Because of the fog, they couldn't land at their home field.

Between telling about the attacks, Henry went through old photos and showed a picture of the girl he dated while

In England, Henry found a girlfriend, Jean Ellery, whose family fed him home-cooked meals.

in England—a pretty lass named Jean Ellery. When asked for more details, he offered that her family lived near King Arthur's retreat.

I ate most of my meals there. She was a good cook. The situation on the English base had big cockroaches. No matter what time I got off flight, she would cook a full meal. Her folks owned a big farm, but a lot of the land was no good. I asked her to come back to the States, but she didn't want to leave her folks. She belonged to the Woman's Land Army. The Cornish people were wonderful people.

A short assignment took him to Casablanca, overflying Italy. One of Henry's photos shows him and some of his crew having a few beers; no Bogart in sight.

Casablanca was hot and sticky, and the people there didn't much care for Americans. The duty there was about the same, except the *Liberator*s [B-24s]had big searchlights. Things were quieting down as the war was most over.

The second time we got shot up is when I got hurt. It was my 104th mission. We got jumped by thirteen JU-88s. We had a crew of thirteen, and only three of us survived [two gunners and Henry]. Some got killed during the attack, and some died when we crashed on the rocks on the tip end of England. We were trying to make a little fighter field. There wasn't much left of the airplane. I saw we were going to crash, so I jumped down onto the catwalk to the bomb bay to shut off the selector valves to the gas tanks. That's the last thing I remember.

That was 1943. After seven months in an Army hospital (306th or 307th) near Coventry, England, for internal damage to the stomach area, Henry went back to the old B-24 unit. But he was grounded because of the injuries, never to fly again.

In the meantime, my clothes got transferred around, and I didn't even have a uniform to put on. They put me in charge of small engines repair and inspection.

We heard most of the war news on the radio. Those Phillips radios were good radios. We got them in the ship's store. The wires were all sealed so the sea water wouldn't bother them. The airplanes all had Helecrafter radios. Ford had the replacement parts contract. Consolidated had built the airplane and sometimes the replacement parts just would not fit. I worked as a machinist mate repairing mostly aircraft equipment until Victory In Europe [V-E] Day.

V-E Day was the biggest Christmas tree in the world. We flew without running lights or anything before that. And that night all the planes were up with all their lights on. So you can imagine all those planes up in the air [with their lights on]. They were as thick as bees.

We came back to the States in forty-four. We landed in Norfolk and then we were sent down to Chincoteague Island, Virginia, but we couldn't stay there because the runways weren't long enough for B-24s. From there we went to an air base near Miami, Florida. It's no longer there. That's where we were when we heard about the atomic bomb being dropped on Japan.

All the boys wanted to celebrate, and they were looking for liquor. I was there about ten months. The skipper there didn't give a damn for the rules. He took a plane for a joy ride—to Cincinnati where his family was. Because of the joy ride, we all got busted, but he was a nice guy. I was discharged at Christmas time in 1945.

Henry described his discharge as "an honorable medical discharge," indicating the military took particular note of the "medical" condition.

I'll tell you about the trick they pulled on us. When we came back, they wouldn't recognize us because we hadn't gone through school [for the flight rating]. Without the rating, it was hard to get promotions. They never did recognize the *AEP*s as pilots.

Henry got a ten percent disability pension and still fights problems created by the crash near England. His separation papers don't reflect any medals, ribbons, or the Purple Heart. With Henry's okay, the local Disabled American Veterans chapter is working to find out why.

Gordon Briggs Of Athol   United States Army Air Corps, 1943-1945

In P-47 Combat Over Belgium, Germany

Gordon Briggs was always interested in flying. He joined the Athol-Orange Aero Club before it was time to go into the military, about 1940. He had graduated from Athol High School in 1939 and then worked at Union Twist Drill (UTD), an Athol manufacturer of drills and cutters. He

house and around the area from the Piper *Cubs* I flew. So my interests were in flying, and when it came close to the time I expected to get my draft notice, I definitely wanted to get into the Army Air Corps, as it was known then, with hopes of becoming a pilot.

Gordon went to the post office in Springfield and took

the minimum. Those that passed the written test were asked to stay over and go to the Springfield hospital the next day to take the physical exam, which I did and I passed. We stripped down to our skivvies and got a thorough exam. During the eye exam, I found out I had 20/15 vision [better than the 20/20 required], and my color tests went far beyond the required range.

About a week later, he was sworn into the Army Air Corps. Then he went down to the draft board to say, "Sorry, Gentlemen. You can't touch me."

I can remember Johnny Johnstone and Mr. [George] Grant down at the draft board. They gave me a hard time with a twinkle in their eyes that said, "another one got away," but, of course, they congratulated me and wished me well and said that they were sorry to lose me but were glad I was going to do what I wanted to do.

Gordon was sworn in about September of 1942 but had to wait for service because so many men had already been accepted and were waiting to be called. The Army couldn't handle them. He went back to UTD to his previous job. Then in January,1943, he got a notice to report for active duty. On 28 January, he went to Springfield with Wallace Chubbock

He named his fighter plane *Polly* in honor of his future wife back home, and **GORDON BRIGGS** experienced flights during World War II that most people would never be able to imagine.

belonged to the Aero Club until he finally got accepted for active duty in the Army in 1943.

I never flew long enough before the war started to get a private license. I did have a solo permit, so I went up by myself and flew around town and the area. I took movies over my

written and physical exams to enter the Air Corps. Some earlier requirements had been eliminated, including one for a college education.

I took a 150-question college equivalency exam, a multiple choice-type test and you had to score a hundred or more to pass. I got quite a bit beyond and two or three others. Once again, he reported to the post office.

From Springfield, they went by train to Atlantic City, New Jersey.

Atlantic City and Miami were the two big reception centers, due to the large number of hotels at each location. Thousands of us were taken in, and we filled most of the major hotels. I was assigned to the Chelsea Hotel. They had decided that because they were losing so many potential pilots to "washing out" in pre-flight training [being eliminated from the flying program] that they would give new recruits some brushing up on their education.

First, we took a month of Army basic training: learning to march, close order drill, gas chamber [tear gas exposure for orientation], shots, and everything else that's part of basic training. When we were learning to march, we went to a small airport near the hotels in Atlantic City. One day, while we were training, a P-47 fighter plane started circling the field as though it wanted to land.

The drill instructors knew that we were potential pilots, so they stopped our marching and let us watch as the P-47 made an approach and came in to land. The field seemed very small for that big plane, and the pilot came in quite high and tried to land. He finally got it down but was too far down the runway to stop it, so he must have really stood on the brakes. The plane nosed over and ended up on its back. We never knew why he tried to land or if

he was hurt, but the Army drill instructors kept ribbing us, like, "See what happens when you fly them things? Do you boys still want to be pilots after seeing that?" I didn't realize then that I would end up flying those same P-47s, and we surely had a rude introduction to them. Then we were

> **The pilot came in quite high and tried to land....The plane nosed over and ended up on its back....I didn't realize then I would end up flying those same P-47s, and we surely had a rude introduction to them.**

dispersed to colleges all over the Northeast down into Virginia and North Carolina, about five hundred to a college, for intensive academic training.

I went to Colby College in Waterville, Maine. We were taught by the regular professors, and we would spend perhaps a day on fractions, a day on decimals. The subjects were taught so fast that within a week we were doing calculus. Colby was not like the Army. Except for the Army restrictions, it was like a country club. We were invited to people's homes for Sunday dinners, and we put on a real "snappy" parade for Waterville on Memorial Day. We had certain things we had to do, but the atmosphere was without doubt the least "Army-like" situation I encountered while in the service.

While at Colby, the Army took potential pilots out to the local airport where they got eight or ten hours in Piper

Cubs with civilian instructors. Since he had already soloed Piper *Cubs*, Gordon enjoyed the outing.

My instructor even fell asleep one time on a hot sunny afternoon. Of course, he knew that I knew how to fly, so he was relaxing while I practiced.

For some of the fellows, it was the first time they had even been up.

You knew who the first timers were when you saw them get a bucket to clean out the plane after they were back on the ground.

He was stationed in Waterville from the beginning of March until 4 July 1943. On the Fourth of July weekend, the Army shipped them from Waterville to Nashville, Tennessee, a three-day trip. Men who had departed a month earlier had gone in tourist sleeper cars.

When we got to the station, all we had were some old coach cars, one of which had a toilet but no sink. We were supposed to get the sleeper cars in Portland, but when we got there, none were found. There were so many civilians traveling on the holiday by train due to the gas shortage, that we went the whole three days in an old coach. We took the backs off the seats and laid them flat so we could sleep.

They hitched us to trains going our way, as we didn't have enough cars to have our own engine. I even came right

On Duty...
Geography
Gordon Briggs

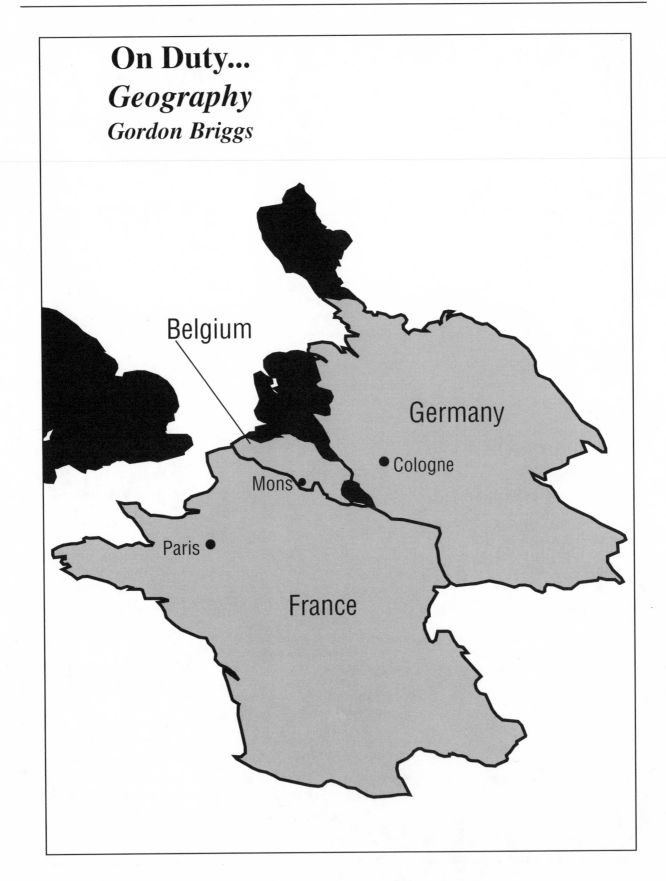

through Athol as we hitched to the *Minute Man* [one of the trains that went through Athol nearly every day on its way to Chicago], but I couldn't get off or let my family know I was coming through. It was a dirty, tough, hard trip. We were glad to get to Nashville, even though it was a lot hotter than Maine.

Nashville was the classification center. They were there about three weeks. That's where they were given the "manipulative test" to check hand-eye coordination to determine what kind of job each was best qualified to do. It seemed that regardless of the test scores, placement depended on what they needed. If they needed pilots, you'd be classified as a pilot. If they needed navigators, you'd be classified as a navigator. Gordon got his wish and was selected for pilot training. His next stop was Maxwell Field in Montgomery, Alabama, for pre-flight training.

At that time, we were finally aviation cadets [they had been called aviation students while in the college training detachments]. We took all the Army insignia off our uniforms and put on the aviation cadet insignia. This caused our heads to increase a hat size or two.

We soon found out just how tough cadet training was. We were there two months, as underclassmen one month and upperclassmen one month. It wasn't as bad for us as it had been for the early guys. We didn't have to walk a rat line or brace or eat a square meal.

Walking a rat line was walking at exaggerated attention, almost in a brace condition taking small steps, no arm swing and staring straight ahead. A brace was pressing flat against a wall so there was no space between the small of the back and the wall while forcing the chin in to create multiple chins. A square meal required the eater to stare straight ahead, pick up the fork, retrieve a bite from the plate, lift the bite vertically to the height of the mouth, and make a square corner as the fork changed direction toward the mouth. The right-angled pattern returned the fork to the plate, where it was placed while the cadet chewed the bite, still staring straight ahead. The process continued throughout the meal. All of those punishments could be administered on a lower classman by an upperclassman, supposedly to test self control.

Fortunately, when I arrived, things had been ordered changed. They needed replacement pilots, so they relaxed the training that was causing some cadets to drop out. It was still plenty tough, and our college training helped a much higher percentage of us to get through the academics, although we still lost a few. We didn't actually fly during pre-flight. We had intensive courses in all the subjects we had studied in college, plus map reading, weather, Morse code [fifteen words a minute required both sending and receiving], aircraft identification, and physical training. Several nights a week, the whole cadet wing would march in Class A uniform [slacks, shirt, and jacket with all hardware: insignia, ribbons, and medals] to the parade ground for retreat ceremonies, including passing in review. That was quite a sight, even if you were marching in the ranks. After two difficult months, those of us who made it went on to primary flight training at different flight schools.

Gordon shipped out of pre-flight on an overnight train to Dorr Field, Arcadia, Florida for primary flight training. Arcadia is a little above Fort Myers, and the field was about twenty five miles from Arcadia, "out in cattle country." It had previously been an Embry-Riddle Flying School that the Air Corps took over. Cadets were issued flight suits, helmets, and goggles. The primary trainer was the PT-17 *Stearman*, an open cockpit biplane with two seats in tandem.

It was a beautiful plane to fly. You wore the helmet and goggles and a scarf. We felt like we were really "hot pilots." We had civilian instructors, and I had one of the older instructors. His initials were GMC, Gordon M. Currier. His pilot license number was very low, indicating he had been flying a long time. The one thing I remember him telling us was, "Men, there are old pilots and there are bold pilots, but there are no old, bold pilots." I was happy to have such an experienced instructor to start me off right. Anything I had learned about flying before, I soon learned, was best forgotten. The Army had its own methods of teaching, and you did it their way or you were gone.

A flyer's log shows information about flights and aircraft: the date of a flight, type of airplane flown, duration of flight, whether local or cross-country, whether day or night, and remarks. Gordon's pilot log shows that his first flight in "primary" was on 5 October 1943. The instructor sat in the front cockpit and the student, in the back. The instructor had a speaking tube in the front, and, in the back, the student plugged the other end into his helmet. "So he could talk to us, but we couldn't talk back to him."

Gordon obviously enjoyed the PT-17.

The *Stearman* was absolutely magnificent the way it handled in the air, and with the wind whistling through the guy wires, it was really fun to fly. Landing was another thing because of the very narrow landing gear, with wheels only six or eight feet apart. If you didn't land directly into the wind, you could ground loop it very easily, or if you didn't slow enough before you turned off the grass landing strip, it could be a problem. Unfortunately, a lot of guys dragged a wing if they weren't careful.

Usually, a dragged wing was enough reason to eliminate the would-be pilot from the program.

It was sad to see someone packing to leave for some other kind of duty. Before we soloed, we had to wear our goggles backwards over the back of our helmets. Every step we took, the goggles would bang us in the back of the head. We were referred to as "Dodos," and it was a real thrill not only to solo and see that empty seat in front of you, but also to be able to move the goggles up to the front of our helmets where they are supposed to be and leave the ranks of the "Dodos." During the month that I was an underclassman, I frequently saw Doug Starrett, now president of the L.S. Starrett Company. He was an upperclassman at that time.

My most vivid recollection in primary flying was after I soloed. My instructor and I went to an auxiliary field. He got out, and I took off. I made three passes around the field, and after the third landing, I taxied back to pick him up. He knew I was a little bit uptight from soloing [although it wasn't my first solo, so it probably wasn't as dramatic for me as for some of the others]. He signaled me that he was flying the plane and to relax. He climbed to about twenty-five hundred feet or so and said, "Is your seat belt tight?"

I said,"Yes." He rolled it over, and we flew upside down for thirty seconds or so.[The *Stearman* had a carburetor that worked upside down without stalling].

When we rolled over and stayed there, I was hanging on to the sides of the cockpit for dear life. There was nothing between me and the ground except that safety belt. He rolled it back over with a grin on his face. We went along a little way, and over he went again. He said "Okay. Let's see your hands." He knew darned well I was hanging on for dear life.

It was important for us to learn to trust that the safety belt would hold us in, because once you started doing maneuvers yourself, you couldn't hang onto the frame. You needed one hand for the stick and one for the throttle. We always made sure when we buckled up to pull the safety belt just as tight as it would go, almost to the point of cutting off the circulation so it would hold us firmly in the seat when we were upside down. When you did a roll, you were upside down briefly. Of course, we always wore a parachute which we sat on, but I never had any parachute training except "This is your ripcord, and this is what you do." And, fortunately, I never needed it. They always guaranteed that if it didn't work, you could bring it back for another—"FREE."

Gordon's pilot's log has recorded 65:01 hours during primary training. Much of that flying was precision aerobatics, such as spins, slow rolls, snap rolls, Immelman turns: all the basic maneuvers. After passing the flight tests, he was sent to basic training at Bainbridge, in the southern part of Georgia. The Air Corps used a low-wing plane with a greenhouse (bubble) canopy, the BT-13. A low wing airplane means that the wings were below the body of the aircraft. BT stood for "basic trainer."

We called it the "Vultee Vibrator." It was built by the Vultee Aircraft Company. It had a 450-horsepower engine with a two-position propeller. There was low pitch used for take off and landing and high pitch for cruising and level flight. In contrast to the *Stearman*, it had a huge wide landing gear. You couldn't ground loop it if you tried. The trouble with that was we got lazy, and when we moved up to the AT-6 with its narrow gear, guys washed out. They'd go to turn off the landing strip too fast and drag a wing tip.

That BT-13 wide gear lulled some into a false sense of security. The BT-13 had movable flaps we would crank down with a lever in the cockpit as we approached for landing. I developed a bad habit of putting my flaps down too soon when coming into the landing pattern. I got away with it until one day when my instructor rode with me. He had warned me about not lowering the flaps above 135 miles per hour, because they could be damaged by the higher air pressure created by higher airspeeds.

As I entered the pattern, I once again started to crank down the flaps at about 145 miles per hour, only that time, the handle wouldn't turn. I realized my instructor had anticipated my bad habit and was holding the flap lever so I couldn't turn it. He didn't say a word, but when we got on the ground and back to the ready room [where we stayed until we were ready to fly], he calmly told me to go up to the blackboard and write as many times as I could fit on the board, "I, Aviation Cadet Gordon Briggs 11099048, will not lower my flaps above 135 miles per hour." After that, I had to meet the next flight returning to the ready room at the door and say the same thing to each of my cadet buddies as they entered the room. It was very embarrassing, to say the least, and from that moment on, my bad habit was broken. They always were able to demonstrate the errors of our ways in a most convincing way.

Basic training was similar to primary, except in a faster, heavier plane and with new maneuvers and tactics.

We started formation flying. The instructor would fly the lead plane and two of us cadets would fly, one on each side of him in a fairly close *V* formation. We had to learn to take off, fly around, and land while staying in that position, looking at him and not looking ahead to see where we were going. The first time you came in and didn't look where you were going, it was a little bit unnerving. You'd have to watch the lead and stay within a certain width from him. Of course,

when he's about to land, you can see the ground under him. You'd come back on the stick and do what he was doing, but it was a little tough not to look straight ahead at where you were going. Also in basic, we started instrument flying, cross country, and night flying. In spite of a lot of bad weather, we managed to get in our required sixty-five hours in that phase of our training.

Basic training lasted from 1 December 1943 until the first part of February, 1944.

I must mention one thing that happened at Bainbridge. One Sunday morning we were lounging in the barracks [we seldom flew on Sunday], and we heard singing like a men's chorus outside. We looked out, and there was a platoon of German prisoners of war being marched to church, swinging along in exact step and singing a German marching song. We were so far removed from the war and so engrossed in our training, it gave us a strange feeling to see the "enemy" in their German uniforms showing us how well trained they were in marching and discipline. In spite of being POWs, they looked very proud, and it was a sight I have never forgotten.

One more phase of flight training was required before the new pilots would be ready to get their wings—advanced flight training. They were sent fifty miles west back into Florida to Marriana for training in the AT-6. The AT-6 was a low wing airplane with a greenhouse canopy, retractable gear, six-hundred horsepower engine, and constant-speed propeller. It was built by North American. The constant-speed prop meant the propeller's pitch would automatically shift to maintain a set speed, sort of like today's automobile cruise controls. Flight lessons were more of the same, except with added mild tactical maneuvers, night cross country, more formation flying, low altitude cross country, and high altitude oxygen missions.

One of the biggest reliefs I got was when the instructor got out of the plane when I checked out in night flying. The cadet sat in the front seat in the AT-6, so the visibility from the back seat was limited, even in daylight. I got a brand new instructor for night flying, and we went around the field several times before he decided to let me go on my own. He was down in a hole in that back seat, and he was yelling. He would get on the controls and interfere with my landings. Of course, I couldn't say anything without getting into deep trouble, so I suffered through until, at last, he decided I was out to do him in. I couldn't wait to get him out of the plane. Finally, he crawled out, and I got to enjoy the flight.

One night, Gordon volunteered to fly planes to an auxiliary field for other cadets to check out in night flying.

We took off, and there was

a full moon. It was so beautiful up there that we flew around awhile until they finally ordered us into the field so they could get their class started. We hated to come down. We were questioned as to why it took us a half hour to get to the field when it should have taken only ten minutes.

Other incidents during advanced training stayed with Gordon. One involved his roommate.

We were doing a night cross country. After everyone else had checked in, we discovered my roommate was missing. We hung around the operations room hoping to hear from him. Finally, we got a phone call that his plane had broken an oil line and he had to bail out. He finally reached a house where he could call the base.

We were very relieved to learn that he was all right, and they sent a jeep to pick him up. We waited until he arrived, and he was carrying his open chute. His clothes were all soaked in oil. He said that he had just turned onto the final leg of the cross country, and he could see the lights of the field on the horizon when, suddenly, everything blacked out. He stuck his head out of the cockpit and felt something on his face and realized it was oil. He knew the engine would shortly quit. You don't make a forced landing at night, so he knew he'd have to bail out.

He grabbed the Form 1 [record of the aircraft's maintenance], stuffed it into his flight jacket, unlocked his safety belt, and went over the side. He landed okay but

walked quite awhile before he found a house where he could call. It was quite an experience for him.

A second incident that impressed Gordon was at night at the mess hall. It happened one night of the week when the married cadets could have their wives on the base for supper. The main course was ham.

Some of the ham was bad, and about 150 of us, including some of the cadet wives and me, got violently ill from food poisoning. I don't think I have ever felt so sick in all my life. Most of us ended up at the base hospital for a day or two until we recovered. We heard that the second lieutenant who was in charge of the mess hall was either demoted or failed to receive a promotion. It was years before I could stand to eat ham again.

To supplement flying, pilots got practice in Link trainers, machines that have the "look and feel" of an airplane and were used for practicing instrument flying. The patterns flown in the simulator were drawn out on charts, so the instructor could evaluate the "flight."

Advanced training was about sixty-five or seventy hours in the AT-6. That took a couple of months, making six months of flight training (two primary, two basic, and two advanced). Gordon's group of cadets started in the fall and graduated in class 44D, in April of 1944.

After advanced training, we were ready to graduate and become "Officers and Gentlemen" by an act of Congress. Most of us were commissioned second lieutenants. We got our wings and commission at the graduation exercises. A few of the pilots, for whatever reason, were made flight officers, a rank below second lieutenant, but they did receive their wings during graduation. It was a very proud and happy day for me, except that none of my family could travel all the way to Florida for the ceremony.

Graduation was followed by a ten-day leave. It was the first leave since Gordon had reported for duty fifteen months earlier. The only transportation to Athol was train. When the leave was over, he took the train back to Florida, to Eglin Field on the Gulf coast.

The first thing we got was gunnery training in the AT-6. It had one thirty-millimeter machine gun that fired through the propeller. The gun was synchronized to fire when the propeller blade was out of the way. As luck would have it, the same second lieutenant I had for night checkout was my instructor for my first gunnery lesson on the AT-6. On the first pass, the gun ran away [the pilot stopped pressing the trigger, but the gun continued to fire]. So I held the nose down. I didn't want to spray the whole area.

He was yelling at me, "Stop firing!" He was pulling back on the stick, just like he was on night flying. Finally, the gun ran out of bullets, so I pulled the nose up and headed back to the field, all the time listening to a tirade coming from the back seat. The main difference was that I was a second lieutenant like him. When we landed and he started to climb all over me, I politely told him the gun had run away, and I was trying to not kill anyone. Fortunately for both of us, I never had to ride with him again.

During the two weeks of gunnery school, Gordon learned to attack ground targets as described above. They also tried aerial gunnery in preparation for air-to-air combat. Basic aerial gunnery is firing at a *sleeve*, a long cloth cone attached to a cable and pulled by another airplane.

For the sleeve targets, we had a certain pattern to fly. You'd come around at an angle, shoot at the sleeve, and break away. You had to learn to lead the sleeve to hit it. You had to be careful not to get too far ahead of the sleeve, because you could hit the plane instead of the target.

After gunnery in the AT-6, Gordon and his group transitioned to the *P-40*. The letter *P* indicated the primary purpose of the aircraft was "pursuit." The earlier "birds" he flew were primarily trainers.

The first time I took off in that combat airplane [P-40] was probably the biggest thrill of my life. It's like getting into a T-6 after flying a Piper *Cub*. There was that much difference. We had several days studying manuals and sitting in the cockpit memorizing everything. We would work in pairs, with one in the cockpit with his eyes shut trying to put his hands on whatever control the other one called out. Finally, after passing a blindfold cockpit check from an instructor, we were ready for our first P-40 solo flight.

The P-40 only had one seat, so the first flight was solo. It was in Florida in May, and it was very hot. The P-40 was a liquid-cooled engine that could easily overheat, so they couldn't practice taxiing.

Once you started the engine, you had only a few minutes to get into the air so there would be enough air passing over the coolant to keep the engine from overheating. When we were ready, strapped into the seat, the ground crew would wind up the inertia starter with the crank. We'd engage the engine, and everyone would scramble out of the way so we could start taxiing. The tower would give use a takeoff check while we were taxiing and trying to watch the taxiway. The minute you got out there, "GO!" If you held it on the ground for more than five or ten minutes, the engine would "detonate" [prefire]. It only happened to me once. I had to cut the throttle and sit there for two hours waiting for the engine to cool down before I could take off again.

The first time we took off, most of us did the same thing: went out of sight after takeoff with wheels still down. You were supposed to climb to five hundred feet and turn out of traffic, but everything happened so fast. The P-40 had an electrically-operated hydraulic system. You pulled the wheel lever up, but that didn't pull the wheels up. You had to hold the little trigger on the button of the stick to activate the hydraulic system. One wheel came up first, and then the other, so it took quite a while to get the wheels up. The first landing I made in the P-40 was a joke. We were used to the AT-6 pattern [which was small and close to the field]. Well, I didn't think how much faster the P-40 was, so I made the same pattern. I didn't even have my flaps down on my first attempt, so the controller said, "Go around." The second time, I backed off another mile or so to give myself some time to get the flaps down and get ready. It was a beautiful plane to fly.

Centrifugal and centripetal forces created as a pilot "yanks and banks" the aircraft through the air are referred to as *G*s. One *G* is the force of gravity. *G* forces can cause the vision to narrow from the sides until a pilot is "looking through a straw." Higher forces can cause a pilot to black out.

I remember, on one flight, I went up to about eighteen thousand feet, rolled it over, and pulled it right through. When I leveled out at the bottom, I was going about 450. It was the fast-

est I ever went. I was stuck right in that seat [by the *G* force], and I grayed out a little bit, but I didn't black out. Often in combat, during violent maneuvers, we would hear everything going on but couldn't see for a few seconds. The blood has to drift back up into your brain before the vision comes back.

After approximately fifteen hours of P-40 flight time, some were selected to train on the P-47 *Thunderbolt* fighter plane. They were sent to Camp Springs Army Air Base at what is now Andrews Field in Washington, D.C. Again, travel was by train.

Before we started transition in the P-47, we were given a chance to check out in the A-36, the Army version of the Douglass *Dauntless* dive bomber that the Navy used so much in the Pacific. We soloed it around the field about three times to help us get the feel of a heavier airplane. It was fairly easy to fly, and it really came in at a steep angle to land.

Gordon and his fellow students learned one lesson about the P-47 before he saw one up close.

They took us out to a mobile control to watch the pilots in the class ahead of us practice landings. While we were watching, one pilot came in and leveled off to land, only he was about thirty feet above the runway. The plane stalled out, and he came down very hard. The controllers were screaming at him to give it full throttle and go around, which he did. His

tail wheel had unlocked from the force of the hard landing, and he veered off the runway. There was a large sloping drainage ditch there, and his plane went down through the ditch and up the other side. [The ditch] acted like a ski jump that vaulted the plane back into the air.

All that time, he had the engine at full throttle, and the plane staggered off over the trees. Finally, we saw him climb up a few miles away. When he came back around to land, everyone was trying to tell him what to do, and I wondered, if I was in his shoes, if I wouldn't just shut the radios off. Anyway, he made it in, and as one of our famous flying expressions goes, "Only he and his laundry man knew how scared he was."

As we got our first look at the P-47, we were in awe of its size and weight. The P-47 was also a single seat airplane, so no one could go up with you. And, again, we spent hours sitting in the cockpit studying the locations of the controls. They did have harnesses, so the instructor could hook himself onto the wing, and we would taxi with them. The big two thousand-horsepower radial air-cooled engine didn't have any overheating problems on the ground.

The instructor could point out this or that instrument, including the needle and ball, artificial horizon, pressures, mixture—the throttle controls were all together on the left quadrant. The stick was between your legs, with the trigger on the back for guns and the button on the top for bombs.

Trim tabs on the wing edge could be adjusted to "smooth" the air flow over the wing. The tabs were controlled by a wheel on the left quadrant.

The trim tabs were down on the left-hand side—not convenient. When we were dive bombing, you'd reach down and have to take your hand off the throttle [to trim the airplane] or you'd have to whip the thing [trim tab wheel] all the way forward before you started the dive. You'd be out of trim when you started the dive, but as you picked up speed, it would come back into trim.

The P-47 was also heavy. It would stall out anywhere from ninety to 110 miles per hour, depending on the load. When you put the gear down, the tail wheel would lock [in the straight ahead position]. It wasn't a full swivel until you pulled the tail wheel release after you got slowed down and wanted to go off onto the taxi strip.

As soon as we finished our transition phase, we were transferred to Millville, New Jersey, for gunnery. The base was out in the bogs, and the mosquitoes were so bad that you had to sleep under netting to prevent them from carrying you off during the night. We learned both ground and aerial gunnery but used only two of the four .50-caliber machine guns that we later used in combat. We also did some high altitude flying, about thirty thousand feet. We breathed pure oxygen, and some of the old engines,even supercharged, ran rough.

On a gunnery mission over the coast, shooting at a long sleeve being towed by a B-26 medium bomber, I shot off the target. I led it too much and hit the cable. All the guys claimed they had perfect scores that day. [If the sleeve were brought back, the number of holes could be counted because the shells were colored-coded. Each aircraft was loaded with shells of one color that would show up on the target].

During another gunnery experience I had at Millville, we went "five-ships": instructor and four students. I was Number 2 or 3 in the flight. When we touched down, we just let it roll, because we had to get out of the way of the guy coming in behind us. As we got two-thirds of the way down the runway, we'd start hitting the brakes. The P-47, with that tremendously wide landing gear couldn't be ground looped, so you could squeal it around all right. So I was rolling down the runway about eighty-five or ninety miles an hour, and I hit the brakes to start to slow down. No brakes!!

The guy ahead of me was clearing, so I wasn't going to hit him, but there was no way I was going to make that taxiway. I let it roll beyond where they were turning off, released the tail wheel, gave it full right rudder, and ran off the hardtop. As soon as that right wheel hit the dirt, it spun me around so I sat facing the runway.

I called the tower and asked for a tow. I must have disturbed their card game. After a half-hour wait, a couple of enlisted men from the ground crew came out with a cleat track ve-

hicle. They were muttering and complaining that I got dirt in their wheels and they were going to have to pull the wheels. I suggested they fix the brakes so I wouldn't have to get them out there, and they should have been glad I didn't wreck their airplane.

On another mission, the tire was flat. I thought at first the gear was collapsing, but it only went down a little bit and rumbled, so I knew the tire was flat. At the speed we landed, when the tire blew, the plane wanted to nose over. I really had to hold back on the stick and brake it. I kept it going as straight as I could. As the plane slowed down, I pulled off on the taxiway.

After Millville, the next assignment was to Richmond, Virginia, where they assembled to be shipped overseas. Then they went to Camp Kilmer, New Jersey, and then to New York (all by train). In New York, they boarded the original *Queen Elizabeth* ship. Boarding took a couple of days. There were twenty-five thousand, including the crew, on board.

When we sailed, they wouldn't let us out on deck, so anyone watching might not suspect the ship was bursting at its seams. We crossed all by ourselves, with no convoy or escort until the very last day before we got into Scotland. Submarines couldn't keep up because the *Queen* could go thirty-four knots, and subs could only do about eighteen knots. And the *Queen* changed course every few minutes. We zig-zagged all the way over.

Off Scotland, we picked up a couple of destroyer escorts, one on each side. It was quite an experience. There were six of us in a single cabin designed with two three-tier bunks. It was so crowded, we had to go outside to change our minds. Some of the enlisted men down in the holds had eight- and ten-tier bunks; they must have had to have safety belts to hold them in. They had to share the cabin; after twelve hours the other shift got the bunks.

We ate twice a day. It took five sittings to feed everyone. I ate at seven-thirty in the morning and four-thirty in the afternoon. The rest of the time, we lived on candy bars. There was a PX [post exchange] on the ship. We would scrounge rolls and cookies from the afternoon meal and have them in the evening. They just couldn't physically feed three meals. By the time they finished the first sitting, they had to start the afternoon meal, so that's all they had time for.

It took about eight days to cross. It was hot as the devil one day. We must have been down around the Azores. It gradually got colder as we moved up toward England. We landed at Greenock, Scotland, a big inland harbor on a river. They had big submarine nets across the river and they closed them as soon as the ship was in. There were a whole bunch of ships, including carriers and the *Queen Mary* in that harbor. They took us off on tenders.

We took the train down to the placement depot receiving area. In a day or two, we were sent to a field in southern England where we stayed a few weeks and received more combat training. Tactics included dropping small bombs off the coast of Wales, the first time we had done dive bombing.

I got one of those war weary jobs again [a tired P-47]. I tried to loop it, because I had never tried that before. I got some altitude, then dove down for speed and pulled up over in an attempted loop. I was right up on my back, and she stalled out, and I started to drop, tail first. The stick was whipping around, banging me in both knees. I grabbed it with both hands and pulled it back while pushing full right rudder. Finally, I got some rudder in and got into a normal spin mode, and I pulled it out. I lost quite a bit of altitude and, after flying around a few minutes, decided to try it again. Three times I tried that. I could never get it over the top. It stalled out every time. I know you can loop a P-47, but I don't know why that plane wouldn't go through. It seemed like a high speed stall. Just as it was about to go over the top, I would lose the whole thing, and it would just drop like a stone.

After that few weeks of transitional training, the unit flew across the Channel to Orly Airport, Paris. Chateau Rothschild had been taken over as a replacement depot, and replacement pilots, including Gordon, waited there for assignments.

While in Paris, I was able to see some of the famous sights: the Eiffel Tower, Cathedral of Notre Dame, the Louvre, and Arc de Triomphe. It was only a few months after the liberation of Paris, and the city was still in somewhat of a turmoil, so I didn't see it under the best of conditions. I was there the day Charles DeGaulle came and relit the eternal flame at the Arc de Triomphe. I was among about a million people. I didn't get very close, but I saw DeGaulle. He was head and shoulders above the crowd, so I got a peek at him.

It was a little scary around Paris, it was so soon after the liberation. You didn't feel safe at night. We usually carried our .45s [a .45-caliber pistol was issued to each flyer] with us. We had qualified with the .45 before we went over, but it's not an easy gun to fire. You could be fifteen yards away and miss the whole target. If you didn't squeeze it smoothly or if you jerked it the least little bit, the bullet would go off. We only did single shots. You're never going to hit more than the first shot. The recoil would bounce your hand right up.

The adventuresome week in Paris was cut short when assignments came down. Gordon was going to the 386th Squadron, 365th Fighter Group, Ninth Air Force, in Belgium. Training was over, and it was time to go to work.

There were five of us who joined the group at the same time, and all but one was in my squadron. We were welcomed by the squadron commander, taken to the barracks to leave our gear, shown around the area, and introduced to our fellow pilots. We could feel a certain coolness in their welcome, but we didn't think much about it then. As we got acquainted and started flying missions and showed them we could do the job, we became fast friends. A few years ago at one of our re-unions, one of the pilots ex-plained it this way: "We had seen so many young replace-ment pilots come and then get shot down after only a few mis-sions that we hesitated to make new friendships too quickly." I came to understand how he and the other "old boys" felt as time went by and I lost some good buddies.

On orientation flights around the area, they learned the rules before starting actual missions. The P-47 was a "tail dragger." It sat on the two main wheels and the tail wheel. In that position, the pilot couldn't see over the en-gine. After everything checked out at the end of the taxiway, they rolled onto the runway in pairs. The leader kept his position relative to the side of the runway, and the wingman, on the right, kept his position relative to the lead. After a couple of weeks, it was time for the first mis-sion.

The first mission I was on, the squadron commander wasn't scheduled, so he said, "Come on. Get your plane. I'll take you on my wing. You won't be involved. You'll just be on the outside looking in." We were following them out, and everything was going fine. It was a sixteen-ship flight, and

the flight commander's radio went out. He couldn't talk to anybody. Major Cornell, the squadron commander, said, "I've got to go lead this flight. Turn around and head back to the field and get your ass out of here."

He broke away to lead the flight, and I headed home. I don't know where the flight leader went, but I never did see him turn for home. I turned a 180 and called our controller for a fix. I saw some planes off in the distance, but I didn't chal-lenge them. They looked sus-piciously like Germans. That was my first experience on combat. I guess they let me count that as a combat mission, although all I did was go home when he told me to.

For normal missions, we took off in what was called fin-gertip formation. If you hold up your left hand, the flight leader is the middle finger, his wingman is on his right, the el-ement leader is on the flight leader's left, and his wingman to his left. Then as we got out closer to the bomb line, we'd spread out so one shot of flak wouldn't take out the whole flight.

Antiaircraft cannon is *fliegerabwehrkanone* in Ger-man. It provided the word *flak*. Is it any wonder it got shortened?

We'd put at least seventy-five yards between planes. Then, if they got a lucky shot on one, it wouldn't take us all out. That was called battle for-mation. The flight leader would at some point call for battle for-mation. If we made a turn, it was difficult strung out like

that, because the flight leader would be up higher. We'd cross over and be on his inside, and after the turn get back into battle formation.

We were flying from Mons, Belgium. Sort of central Bel-gium, sort of New Englandish. It had a long runway, which we needed with the loads we car-ried. There was many a time I saw the end of the runway, and I was still rolling. I'd say the runways averaged from six thousand to seven thousand feet, and we'd use seven-eighths of it before we'd get off, particularly if you had two five-hundred-pound bombs. We even carried one-thousand-pounders, a full load of gas, three thousand rounds of .50 caliber ammunition, and maybe a belly tank.

We took off in formation, so, here again, you weren't look-ing ahead, you were watching your flight leader. You had to stay in relative position to him. You didn't want to go off the runway and make a nasty mess. So you'd watch him, and as he lifted off the ground, you'd come back on the stick. Some-times you'd bounce it and roll a little further and finally get off. As soon as we were sure we were airborne—bingo—up came the wheels. You'd pick up speed without that drag. One guy went off the end of the run-way. He waited just a little too long to make that choice, "Am I going to make it or am I not?" before he chopped the throttle, and he went off the end of the runway. He hit the dirt and ended up over on his back. God only knows why he didn't burn. He had a full load of ammuni-tion and bombs. How did they remove that plane? Very carefully.

That was November, 1944. Through the rest of November and December, Gordon flew dive-bombing and strafing missions. His log notes one mission when he brought home a bomb still hung on the left wing.

I tried every way I could to get it to drop. It was difficult to stay in formation, because the left wing had that extra five hundred pounds out there. When we reached the field, they told me to circle while the rest landed, so I wouldn't prevent the others from landing if I messed up the runway. I came in and made a very soft wheel landing, then gradually let the tail down and rolled to a stop on the runway. I left the plane right there and had the bomb removed before the plane was brought back to our area.

When we had the belly tank, we carried two five-hundred-pound bombs under each wing. We had eight .50-caliber guns. They were synchronized at about 325 yards, that is pointed so all the bullets hit the same place 325 yards in front of the plane. Man, that was a cone of fire! The force would tip a vehicle right over.

A .50-caliber slug is about three or four inches long. We had two armor-piercing, two incendiaries, and a tracer in every five rounds. You could shoot by the tracer, but you really had to aim through the gun sight. If you started shooting too quickly, you'd see two burst, one on each side. As they kicked up the dirt, they'd travel together, and when they hit and

you were on your target, you'd have one awful lot of lead going in there.

I tipped a van over one time. It was on a crowned road. It was a high-top van, and I hit it right in the cone and put it right over. An incredible force.

We carried napalm at times. The petroleum jelly was very scary, that stuff. You could never bring it back to the field.

They captured hundreds of German belly tanks. The Germans deserted them when they left a field in a hurry.

We adapted them for our shackles [the hooks that held the bombs]. Our ground crews filled them full of napalm and hung them on our planes. Each tank was fitted with a fragmentation bomb and an incendiary bomb [to scatter and ignite the jelly]. We took them back and returned their belly tanks. The only trouble was, if we got going over three-twenty-five [325 miles per hour air speed], they'd pull off.

One time, my instructions were to go in and lay napalm down on a big marshaling yard. There were thousands of freight cars in the yard. They figured we might burn something important. So I was making my approach, and I was watching where I was going and not my air speed. I got going just a little bit too fast. Just before I leveled out for the marshaling yard, the bottom left tank pulled off. Of course, with the uneven weight, it started to roll me right over, so I quickly pushed the button to let the other one go. I straightened out to look where the tanks went. The first one

was out in a field and didn't do a thing. The second one hit about two bounces away from a warehouse. I saw it go *boing, boing, splat*. That thing burned all day. I probably did more damage hitting that warehouse than if I had hit the freight cars. We went out later in the afternoon, and that thing was still burning, so I don't know what they had in there. It was a fierce fire.

Sometimes the bomb line, or bomb release point, was only fifteen or twenty minutes from the base. After takeoff, they would contact a ground controller who would have a target assignment—some point that the Germans were defending. Time over target was usually an hour, or until somebody ran low on gas. The first low fuel light to come on (when there were one hundred gallons left) sent everyone home. Mission incidents are still vivid in Gordon's memory.

A favorite German trick was to bury a *Tiger* tank at a crossroad. It was sitting there able to shoot down either road and clobber anything that tried to come up that road. That kept the ground troops from advancing. Our mission would be to knock that tank out. Many times, we'd hit a tank and put it out of commission and you'd see the road fill right up [with Allied forces].

We also blew up a lot of locomotives. If they were under steam and you hit one, it was the biggest geyser you ever saw. You'd fly right through it.

You couldn't duck it. We hit those with .50-calibers. Sometimes the guys would get really diabolical. They would get behind the train and come right up the train and hit them right in the cab and boiler. They never knew what was coming. The biggest wreck I ever saw was when one guy dropped both of his five-hundred-pounders and hit the track about one hundred yards in front of the locomotive. That thing went *blurp-blurp* and really piled up. We figured the least desirable job in Germany was a railroad engineer.

The *Luftwaffe* had already taken their big losses and weren't a big factor for us. They were flying enlisted men as pilots. I got into air-to-air a couple of times, but it was a Mexican standoff. I didn't get hit, and I did hit them, so we went round and round. One minute you're going round with a couple of ME 109s [German fighter planes], and the next minute, they are gone.

One of our guys was fortunate enough to shoot down an early jet. In those days, the jets only had about ten minutes of fuel. They'd take off, go way up high, idle the engine back, and glide, looking for our planes to attack. If they saw a target, they'd try to get it in a dive. If they lost enough altitude, they'd give it some power and go back up again. Our pilot spotted one and closed on it before the jet pilot was aware of him. He gave us a running commentary. We heard, "I'm closing in. I'm firing on him. I got him. I got him."

It was quite exciting. He had just caught him in that lag [get-ting his jet turbines back up to speed]. If the German pilot had seen him coming, he could have thrown the throttle on a little sooner and pulled right away. I think, all told, the Ninth Air Force shot down ten or a dozen by catching them that way.

I got hit one time while strafing locomotives. I was the last one: "tail-end Charlie." My element leader blew up a locomotive and, just as he pulled away, they knew I couldn't shoot, so they piled out of the bunker, the "flak garden" right beside the railroad. So I called in, "Watch out. We're going to get flak."

It started coming up. *Bomm, bomm, bomm.* We were making evasive maneuvers, full throttle and even water injection [a procedure to boost thrust]. I took what was probably a twenty millimeter in my left wheel well and a second round back in the area of the supercharger, behind the cockpit towards the tail. My plane was trailing smoke, but I got it back okay. We landed on a pierced planking strip laid over grass. It wasn't a hard strip. The wheels came down all right, but as I touched down, I realized the left tire was blown. As I rolled down the runway, the planking rolled up in front of me, and I came awfully near to nosing over. I had both feet braced on those pedals.

As soon as I could, I pulled off on the infield and left it there. They were going to total it, but I said I'd hate to lose that plane. It was the one with Polly's name on it. It was one of the faster planes, a *B* model, and it handled beautifully.

I was fortunate the flak didn't cut my hydraulic system, because without hydraulics, you couldn't get both wheels down [The P-47 had a "shrink strut" so that the wheel came up into the wheel well, the strut would relax, and the wheel would extend slightly. Without hydraulics, the wheel would hang up in the wheel housing. A worse condition was when one wheel came down and the second hanged. Without hydraulics, the down wheel wouldn't retract]. So many times [if a plane lost hydraulics], they had to land on one wheel. They'd fly off most of the gas and then come down and land and hold that wing up just as long as they could. Finally, it wouldn't fly any more, the wing would drop, and they'd skid off. They'd bend the prop and tear up the wing tip, but usually they got them without any major damage, so maintenance could get them flying again.

One day, we heard a lot of commotion. The radio was on in the ready room, and you could here the mission going on. One fellow took a twenty millimeter right in the side of his engine. He was smoking, and he had lost some power. He was struggling to get back to the field. We went out and saw him coming. He came straight in and came to a stop. He jumped out of the cockpit and hit the ground running.

They put the fire out and towed it over to our area. It had a great big hole right in the side of the cowling. The cylinders were mangled, and the oil was gone. That's how tough that engine was. With cylinders with no oil, it ran long enough to get him back to the field.

They told me about one fellow before I got over who was strafing over on the French side, and he went down on a mission and got too low and bent the tips of his prop on a sand dune. He had to use water injection to get enough power to get back across the channel. It burned that engine right out, and when he got on the ground at the first field he could, he couldn't even taxi. He didn't have enough engine.

Little notations in Gordon's flight log include "saw a chute," "no EA (enemy aircraft)," "bombed trains in marshaling yard," "dive-bombed marshaling yard, claimed one locomotive," "dive bombed train," "strafed trucks," "one tank damaged," "milk run," and "Bocoo flak." A "milk run" was a mission as easy as delivering milk, and "Bocoo," like the French *beaucoup*, is jargon for "LOTS OF!"

When you saw the white stuff [flak], it was bad enough, but when you saw the black stuff, the 88s—they'd level those sometimes—that was when you wanted to get the heck out of there [German 88mm antiaircraft guns were a terror to Allied pilots and paratroopers].

We had gone out on a mission on an overcast day. I was Number 2, wingman to the flight leader. The flight leader had to abort the mission because his engine was running very rough. So the element leader took over the flight. I moved up into the element leader's slot, and Francis Roman took the Number 2 slot. We got separated from the rest of the squadron. We could hear them, but we couldn't find them. We kept calling but didn't find them before we got to the bomb line, when they told us to drop our bombs because the rest of them were heading home, and we still hadn't found them.

So we armed the bombs, punched the buttons, and let them go. Part way home, we realized Francis still had his bombs, so as we were coming into Belgium, the leader told him to safe the bombs [so they would not explode on impact at landing]. There was a great big field up ahead. He told Francis to go drop them in the field, so Francis dropped down out of the flight. A moment or two later, I heard the explosion. He had the new electric arming device on the plane. He had armed the bombs but hadn't dropped them over the target. To disarm the bombs, he had turned the handle down, but he had forgotten to turn off the new switches. The bombs went armed and blew up.

The blast caught him. He was less than a thousand feet or so. You couldn't be much under three thousand or the blast would get you. I looked down and saw the plane stagger, with smoke coming out all over. He hit, and the plane exploded and spread all over the field. I said Francis couldn't possibly be alive—there wasn't a piece of that plane big enough. But, by gosh, that cockpit stayed intact. He survived. He was terribly beaten up. He didn't have his shoulder harness locked, as you would on takeoff or landing, so his head hit the gun sight. He had a very bad head injury, the stick stabbed him in the chest, and he broke his legs and one arm. He was very badly beaten up.

There was an antiaircraft battalion stationed on the edge of the field. They got him and patched him up as best as they could. They sent him to a medevac [medical evacuation] hospital nearby. After they stabilized him, they flew him to England to a hospital.

By the time we got back to the base, it was dark. When I got out of my plane, the other pilots were looking at me as if they had seen a ghost. They had heard that Number 2 went down, and that was my position on takeoff. Later, we heard Francis was alive but had been unconscious for six weeks. They gave me a plane, and eventually I found the hospital where he had been. He had been shipped home by then, so I didn't get to see him, but I did talk to his doctor. The doctor was interested to know how he got into that condition. Francis survived, married, and had six or seven children.

Gordon stepped aside from the battles for awhile.

I had my appendix out in December of 1944. I was grounded until March 2. Most of our group got sixty-five to seventy missions, but I only flew fifty-two.

When the Battle of "the Bulge" started, their field in Belgium was right in the path of the attack. With very short notice, the squadron was briefed for a mission and, instead of returning to Belgium, they went down to Metz, in the Alsace-Lorraine provinces of France. In a matter of hours, C-47s were loaded with all the gear. Some of the enlisted men went by convoy. They had to get the vehicles there.

We stayed down there until the Battle of "the Bulge" was all resolved, and then we went back up to Belgium. As the Allied forces drove the Germans back into Germany, we moved forward to keep in contact with the action. Eventually, we moved up to Aachen. We were flying over Cologne and out over the Remagen bridge [Ludendorff railroad bridge]. We were out on a mission over Germany beyond the Rhine River the day they took the Remagen bridge.

Coming back, we saw them swarming across the bridge and fanning out on the other side of the river, and we knew there was a little history in the making. It was very strange to see the city of Cologne almost in total ruins, but the cathedral was standing there practically untouched. They never bombed the cathedral. They made sure it didn't get hit. There might have been small arms fire or concussion damage [to the cathedral], but we never had a direct hit on it.

Once or twice, we got nabbed for some escort duty for A-26s. We just flew up above and just watched for planes. It was quite a sight. We normally would see a couple of five-hundreds going off [five-hundred-

pound bombs]. Here were A-26s carrying eight or ten five-hundred-pound bombs apiece. They all went over at once and let those thing go and, I mean, there was considerably more happening on the ground than when we dropped a couple of five-hundreds. The whole ground lit up. It was a tremendous explosion.

And they were just medium bombers. Imagine when the 17s and 24s went over and dropped hundreds of bombs. That [the A-26 drop] was the most explosives I ever saw go off. Near the end of the war, we escorted B-26s. They were fast. We didn't have to slow down for them. A-26s and B-26s actually flew with P-38s sometimes in their formations. I've seen P-38s stationed at our field with A-26s in formation. They flew the same type of formation that we did, probably because they wanted protection and they wanted extra bomb power. The P-38s would take them right in and dump the bombs and protect them coming back. The A-26s could keep up.

The last mission in May was a weather "rece" (weather reconnaissance). There was nothing else to do, so, to get flying time, they'd go out to see what the weather was.

Then we just hung around, keeping our proficiency by flying local flights—just horsing around. It was a very strange feeling to fly over some of the areas where we were getting clobbered just a short time before. We were up there doing slow rolls as peaceful as anything so we could get one more month of flight pay, they let us

get time in an AT-6 in June. That was when we were on our way home, at Rheims. Bob Hope, Jerry Colonna, and all the troupe put on one of those famous shows that night in Rheims, but I missed it, because we left there that afternoon.

From Rheims he took the train to Antwerp, Belgium, the port of embarkation.

We spent about two weeks waiting for a ship to come in, so to speak. We came home on a Victory ship, the *William and Mary*. It carried eighteen hundred men.

Most came home, but the fellows who were new to the group didn't have points enough to go home, so they stayed with the occupation forces. [Points were acquired by time in theater and by the number of missions]. I had plenty of points to come home, so I did. Some of those who stayed got to fly C-47s, flying anything to fill in their time.

On the first day out of Antwerp, we were going out to the Straits of Dover, and I saw a light flashing on the shore, so I looked up and saw our communication officer flashing back. When he stepped away from the light, I realized it was Irving Luscomb, who used to teach in Athol. I sent word up to him by one of the ship's crew, and he came down to see me. I got to go up to his cabin.

Boy, was I a rumor. They knew I was talking to the communication officer. If I had told them we were going to Nome, Alaska, they would have believed me. As luck would have it, we came right into Boston

Harbor. When we landed in Boston, they had boats all over the place, whistles and everything. It was exciting.

Then we went down to Camp Myles Standish, in Taunton. It took us a little longer to get discharged, because they had to change orders. When we left Europe, our orders were to go home, have a thirty-day leave, and reassemble to go to the Pacific. While we were *en route* home, just before we sailed from Antwerp, they dropped The Bomb [atomic bomb on Japan]. We figured we probably wouldn't have to go to the Pacific. We turned gear in at Camp Myles Standish, and on Monday, they shipped us up to Devens [Camp Devens, Massachusetts]. They put all of the officers in a building and said,

"Right now, you must make a decision. You are either going to stay in or you are going to get out. If you stay in, the chances are that within a month or so you'll be back over in Europe in the Army of occupation."

That didn't sound too attractive, having just come home, so most of us got out. Besides, they didn't want single-engine pilots.

During the Korean War, we were living in Worcester. A letter came to my permanent address in Athol. I got a call from Roger King, the assistant postmaster at that time. He said he had a registered letter which had to be delivered to me personally. We drove up. I figured it was orders to go back in. A lot of guys were going back in.

Polly and I were married. I opened the letter with fear. It was a questionnaire about types of planes flown and how much time I had in each type. At the bottom, it asked, "Do you wish to go on active duty at this time?"

I said, "No, thank you, I do not," and sent it back. That was the last I heard from them.

I didn't do any flying after I got out. I could have gotten a commercial license just for the asking, but I didn't do it quickly enough. Polly and I were married right after I got home, and we didn't have a whole lot of money. Besides, I figured I had probably used up quite a bit of my good luck during combat flying. I'm proud I had an opportunity to serve my country.

Peter "Pete" Krustapentus Of Athol   United States Coast Guard, 1942-1945

Beaming Signals, Informing The World

Peter Krustapentus' military experiences started, as did so many in the 1940s, when he heard of the attack on Pearl Harbor.

Six of us always hung around together, bowled together and everything; we really weren't a gang. We'd do things together like go into Carbone's Restaurant, right beside the York Theater on Main Street [in Athol, Massachusetts]. December 7th, we were standing out front. We'd already seen the movie, and all of a sudden, old Nick Scavo, who was the short order cook at Carbone's, came out and

Sending crucial signals from his LST, PETER KRUSTAPENTUS experienced action in the South Pacific that would go down in history.

told us Pearl Harbor just got bombed.

I said "Holy mackerel."

Two or three guys said, "Where the hell is Pearl Harbor?"

I said it was out in the Pacific somewhere. There was confusion.

President Franklin D. Roosevelt came on the radio. Headlines were everywhere. Right after that, conscription started. Everyone that was eligible got signed up and had to go.

Most of my buddies went into the Navy: Tony Casella, Emile Hachey, and Frank Watkevich. I was twenty-one, a little older than those guys, but I was Four-O [a World War II draft classification indicating he was a family provider]. My father had died the year before, and there were still two younger sisters at home, so I was the only provider. I was living at home and working at Union Twist Drill. I was the assistant traffic manager in the shipping room.

My brother was already in the Marines before the war started. I told my mother I hated not to go in. All the boys were in there, all my buddies. Every one of them was gone [into the service]. She said, "Pete, if you want to go, go ahead."

So, I got Billy Roland, my buddy at the Twist Drill, to go [with me] to the Navy recruiter in Boston. We passed the physical test until they examined my teeth. I had seven cavities that I needed filled. They said they had so many

men coming in, they didn't have time to do my teeth. They were taking only the men who didn't need any work, as fast as they could. They couldn't pass me. So, I said, "I guess that's it."

Then my friend said,

> I had seven cavities that I needed filled. They said they had so many men coming in, they didn't have time to do my teeth....So, I said, "I guess that's it."

"Why don't you try the Coast Guard? It's right down the street."

So I did. The recruiter said, "You're in great shape. Are you a boxer?"

I said, "No," but I did have a good body. I played football and all that.

Then he said I had six or seven teeth that had to be filled.

I said, "Oh, no. Not that stuff again."

Then the chief petty officer said, "We could use you" He said, "I'll tell you what. I'll give you two weeks. You go home. Get your teeth fixed."

So, I went home, and right off the bat, I went to see old Doc Talcott. When I told him about going into the Coast Guard he said, "No problem." He took care of me. He later went into the Navy as a full commander because he was a dentist. He filled three teeth one day and two the next, then two the next. When I went back to Boston, the chief had it [my application] right on his desk. He told me to go in and

see the dentist, who said, "Who worked on your teeth?"

When I said *Dr. Talcott,* he said, "Oh, I know him."

So, it was okay. Then the chief came out of his office and said, " We'll call you."

Thus, Pete was accepted into the Coast Guard, but he had to wait a while. There were so many going in at the same time, the boot camps were full. In the meantime, his friend, Billy Roland, went into the Army. After three months, five hundred men got called to go to Boston. Peter was one of them.

We marched in a parade from Constitution Wharf down to South Station with a band and everything. That was a big class. From South Station, we went down to Pennsylvania Station in New York City. There were so many of us, some had to sit on the floor.

So, off we went to boot camp on Manhattan Beach, just the other side of Coney Island. They had just finished the three-story barracks, and they were brand new. We were the first group to go in. We had three buildings of three floors each. We filled that place right up with our five hundred guys. So that's where we had our basic training.

Boot camp is boot camp. The first thing after you got there, you got an examination and then, wham. They gave us shots. I couldn't lift my arm.

We had to wear leggings, dungarees, and blue shirts.

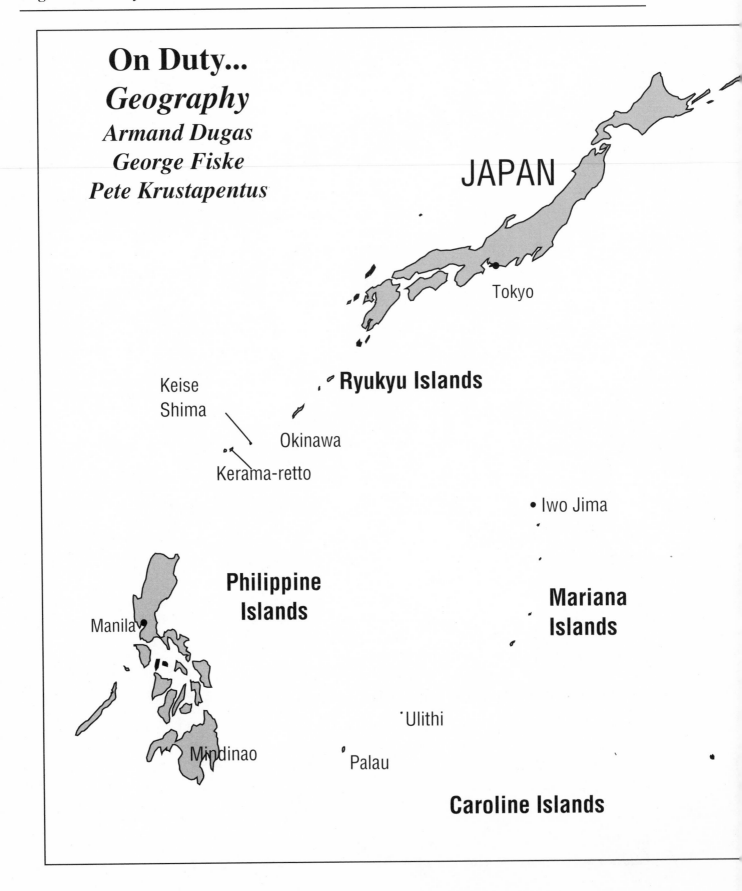

On Duty...
Geography
Armand Dugas
George Fiske
Pete Krustapentus

JAPAN

Tokyo

Keise
Shima

Okinawa

Kerama-retto

Ryukyu Islands

• Iwo Jima

**Philippine
Islands**

Manila

**Mariana
Islands**

Ulithi

Mindinao

Palau

Caroline Islands

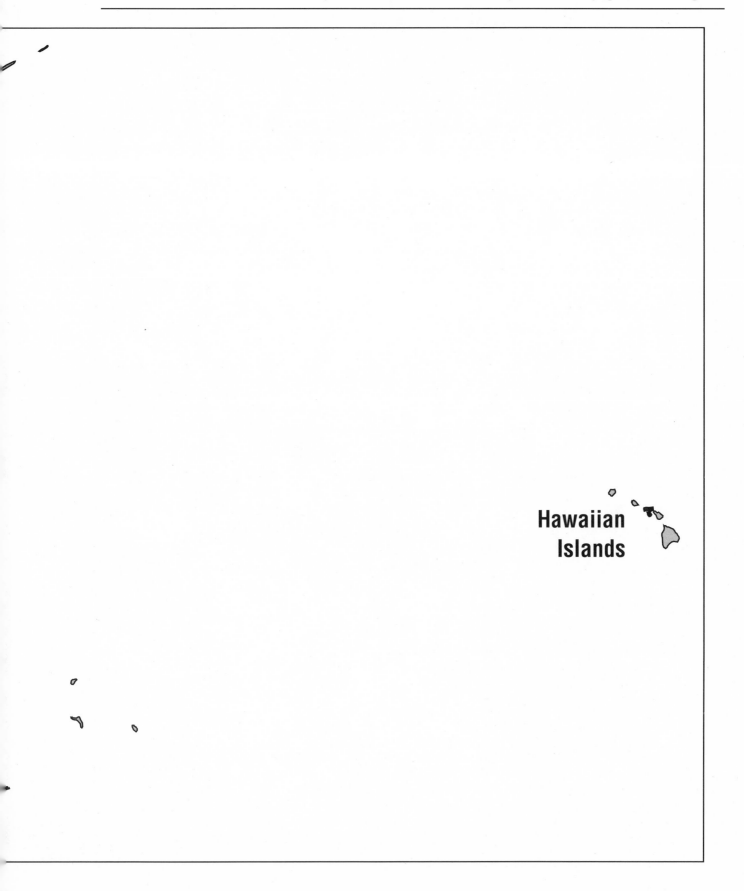

Hawaiian
Islands

Boot camp took about eight weeks. We had to do all the stuff to earn the first class rate. We had to know nomenclature; we had to know ships [silhouettes], flags [signals], and Morse code. We had to do all that stuff.

Plus working your tail off in the galley [kitchen]. There were about six thousand men—in all, eight thousand, counting officers. They had a big galley. I had to wash those big pots. I had that duty for two weeks.

The meals weren't too bad. A typical breakfast was sausage and eggs, a lot of powdered eggs. It was pretty hard to get fresh stuff. Then they had cereals like corn flakes. It was all canned milk or powdered milk. For dinner, you'd have hamburger or sometimes spaghetti or a piece of chicken. Nothing exceptional. We'd get pork chops once in a while. At Thanksgiving and special days, they had a nice meal, turkey and the works. We had a lot of Southerners in our unit. They loved their grits. All the guys from up North used to throw them away. There was a sign that said "Take all you want, but eat all you take." They didn't want any waste. They had to feed a lot of people.

With boot camp completed, Pete was sent to Philadelphia. German submarines off the coast were a concern. PC-45s (130-foot patrol craft) were used as a protective barrier between the cargo ships and the suspected subs.

We'd run patrol to stand guard while they loaded the ammo [ammunition] ships. We had a special card that said we were members of the captain-of-the-port detail. We were stationed at Pier 181, up the Delaware River from the Atlantic. Hog Island is where they would load those *Liberty* ships. Some of them had a thirty-foot draft when loaded [the ship would sink, when loaded, until thirty feet of its height was below water]. They could see the subs in the water and notify the destroyers and cutters, which would go out and throw out depth charges.

A rating meant the sailor had received special training and was more likely to get a promotion. Although he liked the PC-45 duty, Peter had figured out the system and wanted to get a rating. The captain was Lithuanian, like Pete, so Peter thought that might be a good place to start.

I said I'd like to go to school. So he [the captain] sent me to signal school, back to Manhattan Beach. When I got to signal school, I trained for three months and got rated, Signalman Third Class. From there, we had to wait.

While waiting for an assignment, Peter kept a weather eye on the war. The South Pacific was active. Peter followed the news closely.

Right about that time the war planners had the big push in the South Pacific islands. Guadalcanal was one of the first ones. It was the first major battle in 1942, like a preemptive thing. The United States had to get Guadalcanal to keep the Japs from building air bases there. They could have bombed Australia very easily. They lost four cruisers in a night fight off Guadalcanal. The Japs were the best night fighters, and they didn't have radar. That canal off Guadalcanal is called Iron Bottom Bay, because we lost so many ships.

Then they had other things in mind: Tinian, Saipan, Guam.

Following signal school, Peter went via Philadelphia to Cape May Naval Air Station, New Jersey. Fifteen thousand received additional training there at any one time.

After our training there, the big guy came down. He had stripes up the arm and big brushes on his shoulders: an admiral. We had a parade, and he came out and said, "Well, Gentlemen, as of today, you are all in the amphibious."

That was the big push. Everyone went to LCVPs [Landing Craft Vehicle Personnel], LCIs [Landing Craft Infantry], LSTs [Landing Ship Tank]. Everybody was gone within two weeks. I went from Manhattan to Philadelphia, to Baltimore, and to Little Creek, the amphibious training base right across the bay from Norfolk, Virginia. It was rigorous training. We had to go out and swim fifty yards in the damned breakers. Then we got assigned to crews.

Each crew was all Coast Guard or all Navy, but everything else was together. We had a big dummy LST for practice. We didn't really get acquainted with the LST until we took a cruise, a shakedown with a practice ship, off Solomons,

During off-duty hours, Pete, second from left, relaxed with friends, including, from left, Bob Thereau, Emile Sanderson, and Steve Strovisch.

Maryland [a point of land in southern Maryland that juts into Chesapeake Bay]. We lived in Quonset huts, each crew to a hut, usually 130 in a crew. And we carried seven hundred soldiers or Marines, so it was really crowded. The shakedown cruise was up the Potomac, where we made three or four landings. The officers had to learn how to operate the ship.

An LST has an enormous stern anchor. When the ship was between seventy-five and eighty yards off the beach, the crew would drop the anchor and continue on in peeling out the big cable. Once we got up on the beach, we couldn't start the double screws for the simple reason they were in the sand. So we would start the winch and, as we reeled in the cable, we'd pull against that anchor to pull us off the beach.

When qualified to handle the ship, the crew was sent to Neville Island, near Pittsburgh, to the Dravo Shipyard where yard workers were working around the clock building one LST every four weeks.

We went in there and lived at Carnegie Tech at Pittsburgh for four weeks, waiting for our ship. Each day, I went to the shipyard where they were building it. As the signalman, I'd bring all the publications up to date. I was to be the signal man, so I learned all the Navy flags and got training from the communications officer, an ensign.

With a trained crew and a new ship, they headed down Ohio River to Cairo, Indiana, where the Mississippi river joins the Ohio, and then down the Mississippi to New Orleans.

There we got degaussed [some argued that the procedure demagnetized the ship to lessen its potential attraction to mines, while others said it simply allowed the compasses to be properly aligned]. From New Orleans we headed for Guantanamo Bay, Cuba. Part way there, we ran into a hurricane with forty foot waves. So we went back to New Orleans. Finally, the storm stopped, and we headed for the Panama Canal. Going through the canal, you could look up to the top before they pumped the water in. It looked like Tully Mountain [a small mountain near Athol]. Before we started through the canal, I got my first order as a signalman—"Fly Queen."

I said to the quartermaster, "What's that?"

He said, "Fly the quarantine flag." It had to do with diseases in the Canal Zone. We picked up the 6th or 7th Army boys there and took them to San Pedro, California. It took about a day to get through the canal.

The LST docked at San Pedro, discharged the Army troops, and picked up cargo to take to the Pacific, including a LCT [Landing Craft Transport], a small one hundred foot cargo boat. The LCT was loaded on the LST by a large crane.

It made us top heavy and caused big rolls. We dropped that LCT off at Eniwetok.

There was a lot of activity

into and out of Eniwetok. Unknown to the crews bringing in the cargo, the island would eventually become the site of the A-bomb test.

Peter's LST worked its way to Saipan, where they were to pick up supplies and Marines for the invasion of Iwo Jima. His brother, John, was one of the Marines on another LST.

When we came in behind the others [LSTs] my brother spotted our ship number, *789*. He got their signalman to signal me with their light that he was aboard. I used my binoculars to look at his ship and could see him looking at our ship; so I told him on the lights [signal light], to come on over. But that was "No way." The Marines were loaded to ship out for combat, and their commanders weren't about to let one loose without an armed guard. So I told our captain that my brother was on that LST. We were already to go, loaded with Marines. So the captain told me to get one of our Marines to get a small boat, an LCVP, and he gave me a half hour to visit my brother. I hadn't seen him since 1940. We got together, and he introduced me to his friends. There was a guy from Turners Falls. He wanted to give me some of his things, a watch. They didn't know if they'd come back. Kidding around, you know, so I didn't take the watch. But some of them didn't make it back. So then I went back [to my ship], and then we went to Iwo.

At Iwo Jima there was no beach. The cliff went right down to the water. When we went up there, we could butt right up against the cliff and could not even open the tank deck. There was one place, over near Suribachi, where we eventually went in.

Each major battle had its own D-Day. A-, B-, and C-days were planning benchmarks. D-Day was the first day of the battle.

On D-Day we were on Blue Beach. We were Group 86. We were the lead ship, the Group 86 flag ship. There were twenty-four LSTs, all Coast Guard, in Group 86. We got machine-gunned a few times, but you expected that. After D-Day, we took off the wounded to the hospital ships. There were so many dead, the smell was so bad you couldn't even stand it. I can't explain how bad the smell was. Their guns were piled up on the beach. That was when the Japs sent in the mortars.

We had the tank deck doors open and coffee going. Marines came running in and grabbed a cup of coffee. Out they'd go again. One guy with a flamethrower burned three Japs to a crisp, then brought the flamethrower right into the LST to get his coffee. Nobody was feeding those poor suckers. Some of them didn't eat for three or four days.

We spent days taking wounded off. One guy had a bullet in the leg; hit by a forty MM [millimeter] machine gun. We took off the wounded to the hospital ship. Sometimes, we'd make smoke around the hospital ship. Those damned *kamikazes* would come down and strafe the hospital ship, so we'd hide it with smoke.

Probably the most famous World War II photo is one of Marines putting up the American flag on Iwo Jima, to signify triumph over the Japanese enemy. Marines who put up that flag were from the Fifth Division, Twenty-eighth Marines, Peter's brother's unit; although John wasn't there. He had been wounded on the beach going up to Suribachi.

My biggest thrill I got in the whole war was when they unfurled the second flag on Iwo Jima. The first one was on a small pipe [so, for photographic purposes, a second flag was flown. The posed shot made newsreels and news around the world]. We were about a hundred yards away, and I could see it beautifully from my signal position on the LST.

My brother had been shot in the back. He was lying there, and they gave him up for dead. They thought he was shot right through. He was all blood, so they figured they'd take care of the others first. Then my brother said "This is shrapnel. The bullet is still in me."

It just so happened there was another LST that was still in there. It bagged [my brother] off the beach, put him on a PBY [a Navy seaplane with pontoons], and flew him right to Hawaii. He was fourteen weeks in Hawaii in the hospital. It [the story of his wounding] was in the ***Athol Daily News***. The story told about us both being on Iwo Jima at the same time.

After Iwo Jima, the LSTs moved cargo all over the Pacific. One large anchorage that they hit several times was Ulithi, "just south of Guam."

We made an excursion down to New Caledonia and brought back equipment. They were going to build another airfield on Saipan. The next thing you know we were loading up again, for Okinawa. We went back to Leyte and picked up the Tenth Army. They're the ones we brought in on D-Day, the Tenth Army.

We circled around three or four times, made some landings [for practice]. Easter Sunday, we made a landing on Okinawa, and we went right up to Naha. Right up on the rocks. They had a big high wall there, and the guys couldn't get over it. I don't know how they couldn't know the wall was there. But they called the destroyers, who knocked that wall right down. Then all hell broke loose! Five hundred Jap planes came over. It was like a swarm of bees. In the first two hours— and this is no exaggeration— that eight-hundred ship convoy knocked down five hundred Jap planes. The Japs hit quite a few ships, but they didn't sink any. Armand Dugas was on another Coast Guard LST, and his ship got hit with a *kamikaze*—killed two hundred Marines. They were landing when they got hit amid ship. Armand gave up his life jacket because he could swim like a fish anyway.

We stayed there fourteen days. The second night, nearly six hundred Japs were shot down. You wouldn't believe it. We had two twin forties [forty millimeter guns], two single forties, plus twenty millimeters port and starboard. The twin forties were up in the tub [a depression surrounded by armor plating]. They put up a lot of lead. Let me tell you. It was a lot of lead!

I remember one time, it was during high tide. One of the highest tides in the world is on Okinawa. When the tide goes out, it drops forty feet. We were right up on the beach, and I looked back at the ocean, forty feet away. We were up on the rocks. While we were up on the rocks, along comes two *Tonys* [Japanese fighters] strafing the beach. They didn't get too far. We were the second LST in the row. Old Mahalovich, our best gunner, got the first *Tony* with four shots. The same thing with the second one: *blup, blup, blup*. No more. Those *Tonys* were made like paper. If you hit one, it blew up. A *Zero* that had been hit came down about forty yards behind us. We got the splash when it went in.

Then the LCIs came by. They were set up for rockets. You should see them going off. You wouldn't believe it. I don't know how anything could live under all that. The casings covered between forty and fifty yards out into the ocean.

Then, the third day another bunch of Jap airplanes came over, but as time went on, they were fewer and fewer. By the tenth day, there were only thirty or forty. They were coming from mainland Japan. The battleships and bombers had bombed everything on Okinawa. Those battleships lobbed in those shells from those sixteen-inch guns, so there weren't any Jap airfields left.

Back out at sea, Peter's *789* was again moving necessary supplies from safe depots and anchorages to the combat areas.

On D-day plus fourteen, we hit a typhoon. We had a small piano lashed down in a small room used for a library. The lash broke, and there wasn't a piece of piano bigger than the keys. That's how rough it was.

Finally they were back in the safe anchorage of Ulithi, where Pete ran into another Athol Coast Guardsman, Armand Dugas.

He hitched a ride over and came on our ship for a while. His LST was out of action, and he ended up on a DE [destroyer escort].

Guam in the Marianas became a major supply depot after it was secured. The USS *Indianapolis* carried atomic bombs to Tinian, an island just north of Guam. After unloading its secret cargo, the *Indianapolis* docked in Guam's harbor. The crew of the *Indianapolis* was green but had forgone training because of urgent orders to deliver the special cargo to Tinian. Her captain headed for the Philippines to begin training for the invasion of Japan. Of twelve hundred men aboard, barely three hundred ever learned the truth—they had delivered the instrument of surrender.

Nearly nine hundred died at sea.

It [the *Indianapolis*] was right next to us, but we didn't know they had brought The Bomb to Tinian. That's a sad story. After they delivered The Bomb, they took a trip to Tacloban, the personnel transient depot in the Philippines. Three days out of Tinian, they were sunk by a Jap submarine. They had no escort, no nothing.

As Peter and the LST crew were loading on Guam, the Air Force delivered the *Indianapolis*' cargo to Japan. American troops were preparing for the mainland invasion.

We loaded up for the invasion of Japan. We were already loading, had the ammo on and were waiting for the Marines. UPS News Service had a picture of our ship, the *789*, loaded up when the war ended. When I heard it was an atomic bomb, I said, "Holy Jesus." That was really something.

But we continued loading. Then they dropped the second bomb, and we got the message that Japan had quit. We shot off ammo all over. All the lights came on, and it was one hell of a celebration. We stayed in the Pacific moving cargo from Tacloban and Manila to Japan. It was supplies for the occupation forces. We went to Nagoya, Saipan, Pearl Harbor,

and back to Japan. We were there during the signing of the surrender in Tokyo Bay. Finally, we went back through the Panama Canal to New Orleans, where the ship was decommissioned. She was sold to a banana company, and it delivered bananas from South America to the States.

Pete's final thoughts, as he discussed his military career, were of his friends.

One of my best friends, Pete Ringus, went down on the USS *Quincy*. He had enlisted before the war. Billy Roland, the fellow I went to Boston with when we signed up, was dead within eight months. But most of the Athol men came back.

Armand Dugas of Athol   United States Coast Guard, 1943-1946

Outswimming Sharks After Kamikaze *Strike*

Armand Dugas had just turned seventeen and was one of the youngest members of his graduating class from Athol High School. Armand had been an excellent swimmer on the YMCA swim team during high school. Armand, Joe Maroni, Veto Stasiunas, Pat Getchel, Chic Doolan, John Erklund, and others were coached by Bernard "Bernie" Kelley, who later coached swimming at Tufts. Swimming skills would prove to be a life saving asset. That was 1942, and the war was on.

After graduation, I worked at Aubuchon Hardware. I had worked there part-time during high school and went full time when I graduated. It was on

Main Street, Athol, where the Pequoig is now. In the fall of 1942, I went to Springfield with Rusty [Jim Russell]. He enlisted in the Army. He wanted ground under his feet. The Navy was all filled up, so I talked to the Coast Guard. Because I was seventeen, the Navy was in no rush, but the Coast Guard said they would call me.

Armand didn't want to dig foxholes, but he did want to serve. He knew he could be drafted when he turned eighteen, so he insisted on joining the water borne forces.

I went back home and got my parents' signature [required for those under eighteen]. I went back and signed up for the Coast Guard. I didn't get called until March of 1943, but I was

Sharp in Coast Guard whites, ARMAND DUGAS would eventually see Iwo Jima.

frozen [officially committed to service in the Coast Guard], so I couldn't be drafted into the Army.

Basic training for the Coast Guard District was at Manhattan Beach near Coney Island, New York.

It was very, very rigid boot training. The Coast Guard produced a very good sailor. There was heavy emphasis on seamanship: three solid months of training. Seamanship included boat training, lifeboat training, sailing, knots, small-arms training, obstacle courses, and all kinds of drills—very rigid training.

Right next door to Manhattan Beach was the Merchant Marine Academy. We used to meet them out on the seas. Jack Dempsey was a full commander in the Coast Guard, and Gene Tunney was a full commander in the Navy. Boxing was very big. Dempsey used to observe our training, so we did a lot of boxing and judo—a lot of physical conditioning. One day, we were all sparring. I was a southpaw. Dempsey came by, said "Oh, a southpaw," and he feigned a couple of punches.

Out of boot training in June of 1943, Armand went home on leave. Then, he was assigned to be on beach patrol in South Carolina.

We had K9s and horse patrols. They [military strategists] were concerned about people landing on those isolated beaches. Hilton Head Island had been fired on by German U-boats. There was a danger of saboteurs. Then I went

into sub patrol on *Four Hundred* boats, the eighty-three footers. We were operating out of Charleston. I had applied for cutter duty, sea duty. They were into anti-sub work really big. One cutter had sunk a sub by ramming her. On ships, there was the black gang [engine

It was very, very rigid boot training. The Coast Guard produced a very good sailor. There was heavy emphasis on seamanship: three solid months of training.

room personnel], the deck gang [general seaman and gunners], communication gang, commissary gang, and navigation crew. I was a deck man, so I'd do any seaman job it took to man a ship.

Armand never did get into cutters. The Coast Guard was building for the island attacks in the Pacific. Amphibious assault boats was their priority and LSTs (Landing Ship Tank) were high on that list. An LST was 327 feet long and fifty feet wide. It carried a crew of about 125. It would have four decks: the below-water engine room deck, the principle cargo area tank deck, the main deck, and the second deck. The second deck had the crew quarters aft. On each side of the ship the area was divided into large compartments used by the troops.

The call came; I was going to Sullivan Island in Charleston. That was the Coast Guard Receiving Station. From there, I

was reassigned to Camp Bradford, Virginia, for LST amphibious training. I said "LST. What's that?"

They said, "You'll find out, and you're going to have some tough sledding." They painted a "nice" picture.

Camp Bradford was a huge amphibious training base, with two LSTs made of wood to use as training mock-ups. The mock-ups had all gun stations and assigned quarters. Each member of the crew had an assigned area and responsibility.

We had a lot of obstacle course training. That's where our crews were formed, including the officers. We were assigned a Quonset hut as a crew. A crew was between 122 and 134 men. We trained there for three months. Camp Bradford was mostly Navy, but we had quite a few Coast Guard crews there. Each crew was all Navy or all Coast Guard, never mixed. Probably thirty percent of all the LSTs were manned by the Coast Guard. A lot of times, we would travel in the same flotilla. During the final phase of the training, we went out on an LST into Chesapeake Bay. There were two complete crews on each LST, and there were two or three LSTs out there for training. We did gunnery and antiaircraft. We'd shoot at sleeves towed by a tow plane. I admired that pilot who pulled that tow sleeve. He must have screwed up somewhere to get that job. I saw the tow cable get cut not that far behind the plane. And we practiced forty millimeter, double and single, and then twenty millimeters. Every third round was a tracer. I was going for gunner's mate, so I worked as the gunner's striker.

Coast Guard and Navy men could get specialty designations called rates by either attending a formal school or by receiving on-the-job training. Those who tried for the rate via on-the-job training (OJT) were referred to as strikers; they were striking for the rate. An LST had twin forty-millimeter guns in the bow and aft, two single forties fore and aft, and in between, twelve twenty-millimeter guns.

Operating a twenty was a three-man job. You could get by with only one loader, but you really needed two. The forty millimeters had four-round clips. The twenties were drum-fed. Forties would detonate on impact or at around ten thousand feet, but the twenties would only detonate on impact. The twin forties were director-fired. The director had what they called the Mark 14 gyro gun sight. He'd do the whole thing: pointing, leading, every-thing. If the information fed into the sight was good, it was Okay, but if you didn't have the right information, for*get* it. On the twenties, we'd just watch the tracer and try to keep it just ahead of the target.

Fully trained and ready for war, the crew needed its own ship. LSTs were being built by several shipyards. Armand's ship was being built at the

Dravo Shipyard in Pittsburgh, Pennsylvania.

The shipyard was on an island in the Ohio river. Our ship wasn't completed, so we lived at Carnegie Tech, waiting for her to come off. We were assigned two guys to a room; it was heaven. Pete Krustapentus' ship, the *789*, was also built there. Ours was the *884*, so he was there ahead of me. I don't know how many they had in process. They'd lay the keel, then move it up to the next spot; the whole thing was on tracks. Finally, when it got to the final stage, she was launched—sideways. There were 1,051 of those built. That's a lot of LSTs, and there were over two hundred thousand LST sailors.

We were there about two weeks. She had already been launched when we went aboard. The paint was still tacky. No guns were mounted and no masts. The masts wouldn't have fit under some of the bridges when we took it down the rivers. We went down the Ohio to the Mississippi and then to New Orleans. That was quite a trip, going down the rivers. We'd stop at times, waiting for traffic. There was a lot of traffic, barges and everything. They were on a wartime footing. Every ten miles, they'd change the river pilot. The river constantly shifted, and each pilot was responsible of his section. We traveled day and night.

At night, we had huge spotlights on the bow so we could see the shore. They cut holes in the bulkhead large enough to pass a litter through and built a door to go over it so the ship could maintain watertight integrity.

With their brand new ship fully configured for war, the crew headed for the Gulf of Mexico for a shakedown cruise. A stop at Panama City, Florida, got the compasses orientated. Next, the *884* went on to Gulfport, Mississippi.

You never went to the Pacific without carrying a full load. Our ballast tanks were loaded with diesel fuel. We figured we could go around the world seven times if we used everything on board. I think the whole tank deck was beer, bulkhead to bulkhead. We went through the Panama Canal that way. If a ship didn't fit through the canal, it wasn't built in that day. Even the big aircraft carriers were designed to go through the canal. You could see where the sides of the canal were gouged out where a ship had hit it, it was that close.

We put eight LSTs in the lock at the same time. In the locks, we were towed by mechanical donkeys on a track. Each donkey had a winch, and with the cable to the ship, they tried to keep her in the middle of the canal. The LSTs were hooked to each other, so they managed to pull a bunch through together. The LSTs had fenders on the outside so, if they did hit the canal, no damage would be done. Fenders were woven big nets. That was one of the seaman's duties when there was nothing else to do, making fenders. You go through a series of locks up to a lake in the middle. You go through the lake under your own power. It was fresh water, and I remember hosing down the ship. The paint lasts a lot longer if you can keep the salt off. And I can remember crocodiles on the shore. A series of locks at the other end lowers the ship to the Pacific sea level.

Into the Pacific, most ships stopped at a west coast station before sailing into the combat zone. Armand's ship stopped at San Diego, California. With a few minor crew adjustments to leave a couple of men with chronic seasickness and to pick up radio men, the *884* headed for Pearl Harbor. An LST only traveled about ten knots per hour, so the crossing was in a convoy protected by sub chasers and destroyers.

Out of Pearl, we got a couple of milk runs: Eniwetok and back to Pearl. Saipan had been taken, and they were building the fields there. We thought we were to bring supplies there. We didn't know it, but the plans for the Iwo invasion had started.

One day another LST ran aground. She was loaded up with Marines for the Iwo invasion. She was loaded with amtracs [amphibious tracked vehicles] and high octane gas. The Marines were really ripped. They had all their personal things stashed on those vehicles. Our skipper, Pierson, was a mustang [an officer who came up through the enlisted ranks], and he was gung-ho. He jumped in: "My crew is ready." We got loaded with an identical load, and the guys [unhappy Marines] came aboard. We hit a few islands [for practice] meandering our way to Saipan. Big things were happening.

On 19 February 1945, the invasion of Iwo Jima started.

We were out about three days from Saipan before we were told we were going to Iwo Jima. We had Marines who specialized in demolition. The B-24s had bombed and the battle ships had bombarded Iwo for seventy-five days, battle ships including the *Missouri*, the *Arkansas*, the *New York*. One night, we were between the *Missouri* and Iwo. She had those sixteens firing salvos. You could actually see the sixteen-inch shells going right over us. The vibration was tremendous. The whole ship would shake. You could see the big red ball of fire going in point blank. The LCPs [Landing Craft Personnel] equipped with rocket launchers had softened the beach. You wouldn't think a fly could live through that. The whole thing was just a mass of detonations. But they [the Japanese defenders] had pillboxes that had walls that weren't penetrated by direct hits from torpedoes from our bombers. The only way they [American troops] finally got those pillboxes was with flame throwers. They had to cook them [Japanese personnel inside the pillboxes].

We tried to get in during the invasion on the first day, but there was no way. Traffic was too heavy, and the beach wasn't that big. We had a mock-up of the island on the ship. The beach was divided into three sectors: Red, Green, and Blue. And then each color was subdivided into One, Two, Three, and Four. Red beach was nearest Suribachi. The demolition men were really needed, so we went into Red beach that night.

Then we went out for our next assignment. There were cargo ships out there. We were loaded mostly with ammunition and high octane gas. That's what was needed desperately. We would go in, dump a load, and go back [to the ships] for more. We must have gone in and out of there six times.

The beach wasn't secure, and some of the fuel dumps were blown. We were under constant air attack. Iwo is only 350 miles from the mainland of Japan. We were on their front doorstep. Just up above us was the Jap airfield, Chidori [Airfield Number 1]. The wreckage from the Jap planes made a barrier. It was a tangled mass of wreckage. You could stare right up at it. There were terraces of pill boxes connected by underground tunnels. Mount Suribachi had guns mounted on tracks inside. They would roll them out, fire, and roll them back in. One night, we spent the whole night just banging away at the openings with our forty-millimeters. We'd flash a spotlight quick to get a fix and we'd open up: *KaBoomb, KaBoomb, KaBoomb*—just kept pumping rounds into that tunnel.

On Day 4, the Fifth Marines took Mount Suribachi. The famous flag-raising picture was preceded by a less well-publicized actual first.

I remember looking up and seeing an American flag up on top, but I don't know whether it was the first one or a later one. As the crow flies, we were probably between a quarter and a half mile off the beach. Suribachi wasn't that high. It was prominent, because it was the only high point in the area.

On the beach at Iwo Jima, the Landing Ship Tank (LST) *884* was among thousands of land-, sea-, and aircraft that participated in the famous offensive that helped turn the tide towards the Allies in the South Pacific. Armand was part of the *884* crew.

The whole island was shaped like a pork chop with Suribachi at the narrow end. The mountain goes right up from the ocean. So, we were maybe a half mile from the flag.

Divine Wind, *kamikazes*, played an important role in the war in the Pacific and a very personal role for Armand. His first encounter with those suicide pilots was only a prelude of what was to come.

One day, we were waiting for our assignment. We were rendezvousing, circling the volcano island that looked like the end of a watermelon sticking out of the ocean. We could see an observation shack right on the top of it. We were about an hour out of Iwo. Iwo was just out of sight. It took about an hour to go around the island. There was a DD [destroyer with five-inch turrets] screening for us. Chris, the former owner of Tool Town Pizza in Athol, was on that DD.

Five Jap fighters came in from behind the rock, so radar couldn't pick them up. One crashed into a big floating machine shop right across from us about two or three hundred yards away. "General quarters" [ordering all hands to battle sta-tions] was sounding. I came up from below through a hatch that wasn't far from my gun. I saw that ship burning and won-dered what had hit it. The next thing I knew, the LST directly behind us went up. I looked up, and the other three *kamikazes* were making a swing around us just out of gun range. We were training on them.

When you're on a gun sta-tion, you cover a sector. Your gun has a cam so you can't hit your own ship. All of a sudden, they made a swing to the back of the convoy. In the meantime, the other two ships were burn-ing fiercely. One of the *kami-kazes* peeled off and came in directly at us, coming up the convoy, strafing. He got directly over us, pulled up, and dropped a bomb. He just missed us off the bow. Our forward guns had zeroed in on him, and we had him. He was our first kill. The other two *Zeros* went around us once more and headed toward Iwo. They did okay. They lost three of their five planes and pilots but got two of our ships and crews. We took heavy casualties.

As the Iwo Jima battle continued, the traffic in and out eased but the area was still hot. Night landings were highlighted by constant American flares.

There were always two or three flares coming down in parachutes, and they were bright. One night, we were in close. There must have been about forty ships involved. We were about a mile off the beach. All of a sudden, "general quarters" sounded. Our skipper said, "Hold your fire," and he ordered the smoke generators turned on. There was very little wind—actually there was a little fog. It was perfect conditions for smoke cover. There were gently rolling seas. There we were, another LST nudging up against us. We were talking back and forth. The skipper ordered no firing because the Japs could follow our tracers back to the ship. Then we heard a *Betty* bomber come lumbering over us. It was probably about one hundred feet off the water. We could just barely make it out. It started dropping bombs but he got no hits.

Another night, on the ninth day of the battle, the Japs really opened up on the ships that were off shore. We were up close and took a hit. There was a lot of shrapnel clackety-banging all over. Nobody went on the weather deck that night. When we went to the gun tubs, we stayed low. All of a sudden there was a *KaThunk*. We took a hit. The shell went through the hull and knocked out one of our engines. On the tenth day, we left Iwo in a convoy of crippled ships, probably a dozen, headed for Saipan. Some ships could hardly go. It took days for us to get there.

The battle for Okinawa was scheduled to begin 1 April. Rapid repairs made at the dry dock in Saipan got the *884* back into the fray.

As soon as we got out of dry dock, we loaded remnants of the Second Marine Division. We went on maneuver on Tinian to practice landings. We headed for Okinawa. We had twelve tanks on the tank deck, and vehicles covered the main deck. There were two airplanes still in their crates. We called them "flying Jeeps," and they were used for observation. The night before the invasion, we could see the flashes from the battleships banging away to soften Okinawa up.

Prior to the "real" attack on Okinawa, the American forces feigned an attacked in a different area to confuse the Japanese defenders. Keramaretto, west of Okinawa in the Ryukyu Islands chain, had been secured. The island group provided a secure harbor for more than fifty large ships, and they could refuel and replenish for the attack The plan was to have the *884* with its cargo and the Second Marine Division land on the beach after the initial attack.

There was a name for the fake push: Demonstration Group. We had to make it appear like it was the actual landing. It was still dark, just prior to dawn. We had skeleton gun crews out. Everybody was doing last minute things; getting a bite to eat, getting coffee. We knew we had a busy day ahead. I had just finished my coffee and was back at my gun. It was just beginning to crack dawn.

All of a sudden, out of the black part of the sky, I could see ack-ack. At first, I could see tracers going up and converging. We knew there were airplanes coming in, but they were still way off. "General quarters" sounded. Everyone scrambled to their guns. We were one hundred percent manned [every gun had a crew]. They [the Japanese attackers] were coming in on our port [left]. The ack-ack was getting closer. Finally, there were two of them [Japanese airplanes] coming right at us.

We opened up. We got one, but the other one kept coming. I could see the fire on the leading edge of his wings [the aircraft cannons firing]. I could almost swear I could see the pilot. They were *Judy* fighters [a style of Japanese fighter aircraft with an "inline" engine and pointed nose]. He hit just above the water line on the port side, right amidships. It was about fifty feet away from me. I was waiting for the big explosion. I figured, "This is it."

There was hardly a jar when that thing went through us. He was in a dive. We figured he was going four hundred miles an hour. Those *Judys* each carried two two-hundred-pound bombs. One of them went down the shaft into the engine room. The guys down there saw it was a bomb [it didn't explode because it was never released, although internal explosions would soon rock the *884*]. The guys came out of there, and that's what saved them.

The ship started exploding internally. Our bulkheads were lined with ammunition. When that ammo started exploding, the men in the engine room would have been sealed off. We got credit for two Jap planes that day, but one of them got us. We stayed aboard for about twenty minutes. Finally it got so bad, the soles of our shoes were melting. The whole tank deck [the deck below the main deck] was an inferno. The skipper gave the order, "Prepare to abandon ship." I scrambled for the bow.

I saw Marines going over the side with full packs. They sunk like rocks. There was panic. I started telling them to get rid of the packs; lighten up. I told them to unlace their shoes, but leave them on [a procedure that was supposed to give maximum advantage if you encountered a shark]. Those were shark-infested waters. We didn't know how it would help [keeping shoes on], but we did what we were told. Everybody had a Mae West [inflatable life preserver].

Each sailor wore a life belt that created a tube around his waist when it was inflated. As the group formed around Armand, some of the Marines had no life preservers. Armand took his off and laid it out for the others.

There was a lot of panic. Some Marines were getting tired. It was an easy thing for me to do. I just laid [the belt] out flat, and it provided a little added buoyancy. it gave them that little extra confidence. Finally, we got the "Abandon ship," and I just took a dive. I was swimming away. The ship burned. There were a lot of internal explosions, but it never sunk. The ship had been buttoned up [all watertight hatches were closed], but I thought it was going to go over. It took water where the plane hit, and you could almost drive a Mack truck through it. I must have gotten away about a quarter of a mile [to avoid the potential down draft]. Men started to form groups, and there were fourteen or fifteen around me. I could see heads bobbing all over the place. Nobody was picking us up, because we were under attack. No one wanted to stop.

In the meantime, I could see the smoke screen being laid down [for the real American attack]. There was all sorts of activity going on. All the time, the tide was carrying us toward the shore. We knew our forces weren't going to land there, and the Japs were there. All of a sudden, this Navy tug comes toward us. Tugs were in the area in case an LST got stranded on the beach and needed an assist. They were very powerful—big Navy seagoing tugs. They had deck equipment for fighting fires, and they had orders. They went right through us. I don't know how many guys got dragged right down through the screws.

I was digging my nails into the hull. [After an hour in the water, Armand was clawing at the tug's metal hull, trying to hold on in the turbulence.] We were screaming bloody murder. The men on deck of the tug were standing there gawking at us. Finally, they stopped engines and backed down. When they backed down, they washed bodies up forward. The undertow created by the screws on those tugs was unbelievable. So, then, they threw us a heaving line. A heaving line is like a clothesline designed to pull a heavier mooring line to the dock when tying up. We dangled on that, and it snapped. Finally, they threw a Jacob's ladder over the side. We had been in the water an hour to an hour and a half. We scrambled up the Jacob's ladder like dead fish coming out of the water. I'll never forget it.

When we got up, the sun was up. It was April 1, 1945, April Fool's Day and Easter Sunday. We were on the fantail of that tug. We were lying there getting dried out. There was still a lot of action going on around us, a lot of ack-ack. I was stretched out on the wooden fantail trying to get dried out. The sun felt good. I was staring up at the sky, and there was a Jap plane up there just banking around. I could see the meatballs on the wings [Japanese logos of a rising sun]. Nobody was firing at it. All of a sudden, everybody spotted it at the same time. All different

Some time after the LST *884* was damaged by a *kamikaze* hit, rested survivors lined up on deck. Armand can be found five rows back, without a hat, almost directly behind a flag salvaged by the crew.

ships fired at it. The cone of fire was unbelievable. Pretty soon, a wing came off. The plane started spiralling down.

There was an LST about a hundred yards away from us. It looked like the pilot was trying to crash it into that LST, but he had no real control. I could see guys coming out of their gun tubs. They looked like ants. The plane just missed. It splashed a few feet away from that LST. While that was going on, a tanker got hit. A column of black smoke went up all day. By this time, the real landing had already taken place, and our ships were pulling back out to sea. I heard the real attack went in almost unopposed for awhile.

Firefighters poured water on the *884* and "almost sunk it." A repair ship came along side and welded a huge plate over the hole. Kerama-retto also served as a safe harbor for crippled ships. The *884* was towed there. The bodies, mostly Marines, were still aboard.

We buried a lot of people at Kerama-retto. I remember collecting dog tags. You couldn't recognize the faces. Most of the casualities were Marines. We lost four or five guys of our crew. Survivors got picked up by other ships. We never did get an accurate count.

Live ammo in unknown condition was still loose in the LST *884*, so the ship was off limits except for getting the bodies off and a skeleton crew for security. The crew lived on another less-damaged LST and got their meals aboard a damaged heavy cruiser that later gained fame, the *Indianapolis*. On 12 April, a big tug hooked onto the LST being used for their living quarters and started the long journey to Pearl.

They hooked our ship to the LST we were living on and towed us in tandem. The ship we were on had no engines but was otherwise okay, and our ship was totally dead—burned out.

We were leaving Okinawa when we heard Roosevelt had passed away and Truman was President. The flags were at half mast, and we had a little ceremony for the Commander-in-Chief.

We first got towed to Ulithi. We hit heavy seas. The cables between the two ship were two to three hundred yards long. The cable was about three inches in diameter and would be stretched like a fiddle string when we hit a big wave. The LST had a bridle for the cable. There were all kinds of possibilities for collision in heavy seas. As long as the tug kept under way, it was okay. We were right off the island of Truk when the cable from the tug to our LST parted. All night long, we were drifting. Huck, one of our crew, from the conning tower could almost imagine Japs on Truk. The next day, we worked feverishly. The LST we were on was a Navy ship, but it was our skipper who had the deck hands splice another cable as a counterweight. He had little compassion for his crew, but he was smart. We loaded that cable on LCVPs. There were about eight guys on two LCVPs. The weight of that cable almost sank them; their bilge pumps were working overtime. They got the thing hooked up, and, with that counterweight, there was no more problem. We kind of bragged that it took the Coast Guard to solve the problem.

Finally safe in Ulithi, Armand was temporarily assigned to a troop transport, the USS *Randall*, an attack transport.

Ulithi was the biggest anchorage in the Pacific. One night a *Charlie* [solo *kamikaze*] tried to attack the fleet and got shot down. They brought the pilot aboard the *Randall* because it had a real brig. If we could have gotten our hands on the SOB, we'd have killed him. They had him under heavy guard. The survivors of the *884* were not too pleased.

MogMog Island is one of the small islands in the Ulithi Group. It was the R and R [rest and relaxation] spot between battles. MogMog natives had been removed, and the whole island was one constant beer party.

We went ashore for a beer party. They gave each man a case of beer, which is a lot of beer even though it was 3.2. After not having a drink for I don't know how many months, we got hammered. It was a sandy island and right in the middle was a bandstand. There was a band playing. We were in heaven. Fights broke out between different crews. We dragged back to the ship badly hung over. That was the one and only liberty I had. While at Ulithi, aboard the *Randall*, I was lucky to meet sailors from Athol: Joe Maroni [of Athol] from LST *45* and Pete Krustapentus [of Athol] from LST *789*. I had a chance to go aboard their respective ships for a hometown mini reunion.

Two more months of dragging the dead hulk of the *884* finally brought the crew back to Pearl Harbor.

They tied us up at Wapio Point, West Lock, Pearl Harbor; near where the USS *Arizona* is still on the bottom. While I was there, I ran an LCVP. We lived in tents, and we were so happy just to be forgotten. Right next door, there was a CB [construction battalion], and they took us under their wing. That's where we ate. They had USO shows. We loved it. Our only duty was to keep a watch on the hull of our ship. There were still bodies on it. One day, an LST pulled into Pearl and tied up to the hulk of our ship. Don Hager [of Athol] was on that one. He went aboard our ship and took some pictures.

The soft life was not to be. Armand was soon reassigned to a DE (destroyer escort).

In came two big trucks. "Okay, you guys get aboard." We left only twelve guys to watch the ship—it was still commissioned. The rest of us wound up on Pier 11 in Honolulu, at the Coast Guard Receiving Station. We got reissued a whole new sea bag. While I was at Pier 11, the war ended, and that's also when we heard about the *Indianapolis*.

After being repaired at Kerama-retto, the *Indianapolis* went to Mare Island, California, for further repairs and to pick up a top-secret load. From San Francisco, she carried it at flank speed to Tinian. After off-loading her special cargo on 26 July, the *Indianapolis* sailed for Leyte in the Philippines to train for the anticipated invasion of Japan. Three days out of Tinian, she was sunk by a Japanese submarine. Of the entire crew of twelve hundred, barely three hundred men found out they had delivered the A-bombs that would end the war.

Four Coast Guard-manned DEs (destroyer escorts) were in Pearl, all under-manned.

I was assigned to the USS *Poole (DE 151)*. We headed for Japan, escorting the first occupation troops and were in Wakayama Bay when the peace treaty was signed. I was a helmsman on the DE, a dream job compared to the LST. We worked four [hours] on and eight, off. When things quieted down, we cruised back through the canal [Panama] to Charleston, North Carolina, and then on to Jacksonville where the ship was decommissioned and mothballed. I was discharged in March, 1946.

Richard J. Chase Of Athol   **United States Marine Corps, 1943-1945**

At Tail Gun In A South Pacific Dive Bomber

I was in my sophomore year at the University of New Hampshire when the war started. A lot of guys at that time wanted to enlist. My mother would hear nothing of that. She wanted me to finish up the year, which I did. After that, I went to the recruiting station in Claremont, New Hampshire, to sign up. A couple of my buddies had enlisted in the Marine Corps right after December 7 [when the Japanese bombed United States ships at Pearl Harbor, Honolulu, and provoked involvement in World War II]. They were my inspiration to join the Marines, gung-ho and like that. The recruiting sergeant there told me, because I had two years of college, I'd be a good candidate for OCS [Officer Candidate School]. He suggested I enlist anyway [even though it would not lead directly to being an officer].

The Marine headquarters was in Manchester, so I went there. They paid my transportation to Boston. The only exam I can recall was the physical in Boston. We went by train from there to South Carolina. They sent me to Parris Island, where I took basic training. Basic was lots and lots of

Out on the wing of the Douglass *Dauntless* dive bomber he worked as gunner through forty-three combat missions, DICK CHASE was more accustomed to riding in the back seat, headed straight down.

marching and long hikes with full regalia and backpacks. It was mostly physical work, but there were some classroom studies on the basics of military law and discipline. Parris Island had a reputation for being a pretty tough place.

We didn't lose many during training. We were all enlisted men who had some prior knowledge of military training, the history, and tradition of the Corps. We knew it meant instant obedience and that sort of stuff. There was quite a bit of harassment. I smartened up—learned I shouldn't call myself a college boy. "College boys" got too many important assignments like cleaning the latrine. I wised up to that pretty fast and got through basic training without problems.

From there, we went to New River, what is now Camp

Lejeune. That's where we got gunnery and infantry training. That was basic Marine gunnery: rifle, machine gun, mortars, and pistol; not aerial gunnery. I think we were there about four weeks.

By virtue of the fact that I was a college boy, they sent me to Cherry Point, North Carolina, the east coast Marine Air Station. I was waiting for an assignment to officers training school. We were in what was called "casual status." That meant that they handed you a stick with a nail on the end of it and a can, and you spent most of the day picking up cigarette butts and candy wrappers. I took that for a few weeks. That wasn't very inspiring.

I happened to notice a posting on the bulletin board that they were accepting volunteers for aerial gunners. I thought that was preferable to what I was doing.

They put me through a lot of classroom work such as aircraft identification, radio communications, Morse code sending and receiving, semaphore, and how to handle the radios. We did have to learn the basics of semaphore flag communication, but we never used it. I did learn Morse code well enough to pass the requirements. There was a keyboard in the gunner's cockpit, but I didn't have to use it. We never got far enough away from home base to need it. We had just one radio, but it had different blocks for different frequencies. They looked like the old fashioned blocks from a Model-T Ford. There was a trailing antenna, a wire with a knob on the end in the back of the airplane. It could be

reeled out to make an antenna and increase the reception distance. We could tune in the Japanese stations and Tokyo Rose [a Japanese radio voice always trying to dish propaganda against the U.S. or undermine United States troops]. We'd change frequency each

> **As soon as I finished radio school, I was assigned to a squadron. We went up to a small field called Peter Point Field. I was assigned to an SBD dive bomber— that stands for *Scout* bomber built by the Douglass Aircraft Company.**

day to keep the Japanese from using our signals.

Art Howard, one of the gunners in Dick's outfit, notes the date of transfer to Peter Point as 7 March 1943.

As soon as I finished radio school, I was assigned to a squadron. We went up to a small field called Peter Point Field. I was assigned to an SBD dive bomber—that stands for *Scout* bomber built by Douglass Aircraft Company. It was called the Douglass *Dauntless.*

The Douglass *Dauntless* SBD-4 dive bomber was, at the beginning of the Pacific war, the mainstay of the United States Navy and Marine air forces. It was powered by a twelve-hundred horsepower engine. According to Howard, the 331st Scout Bombing Squadron, Dick

Chase's unit, was formed 8 January 1943 as part of the Third Marine Air Wing.

The field was on the coast of North Carolina. The Marines had acquired control of a couple of small islands on the coast where we practiced bombing. The bombs were little bitsy lead practice bombs with a little black powder. They would make smoke so we could check the accuracy [of the bomb drop]. We practiced bombing and strafing. The pilot could strafe with the .50-caliber guns that were mounted under the engine cowl and fired through the propeller. Firing was synchronized with the propellers so you wouldn't shoot the propeller off. I practiced strafing with the twin .30-caliber guns. I strafed with the thirties mostly on the pullout [shooting backward as the plane pulled up from a dive].

We practiced low-altitude flying called hedge hopping. We practiced diving from different altitudes. The SBD wouldn't go very high. The maximum height was maybe twenty-two thousand feet. Even at twenty thousand feet, you had to use oxygen. Most of our combat raids would start from ten thousand or five thousand feet. If we started from five thousand feet, we'd pull out at two thousand. If we started at ten thousand feet, we'd pull out a little higher.

Dick's log shows a different pilot for each of his training flights. Later, when they were going overseas, pilot and gunner were paired. Dick was paired with Frederick L.

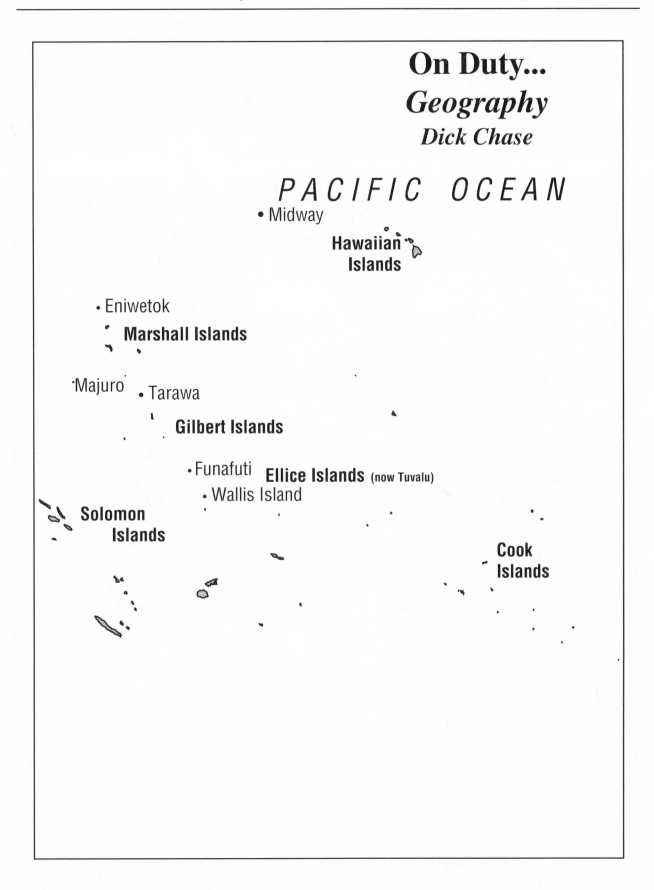

On Duty...
Geography
Dick Chase

PACIFIC OCEAN

• Midway

Hawaiian Islands

• Eniwetok

Marshall Islands

Majuro   • Tarawa

Gilbert Islands

• Funafuti   **Ellice Islands** (now Tuvalu)

• Wallis Island

Solomon Islands

Cook Islands

Doyle, who was to be his pilot during the Pacific tour. Most of the training flights were approximately one hour. The log shows they were flying from Bogue Field, near Cherry Point.

We got quite a few hurricane scares there. When that happened, we had to ferry the squadron to Columbia, South Carolina.

One test hop was to an altitude of twenty-two thousand feet. We had to use oxygen. A test hop was to check out systems of the airplane that had been worked on by the maintenance crews.

We always bombed in squadron formation. That was sometimes a dozen planes in echelon formation, a *V*-formation. The lead squadron would go in first. The others would follow in at different elevations. You'd come in at an angle and level off to get on target. There was a big hazard of rolling over if you made too big a correction. I'll tell you about that later.

From New River, we went to San Diego, where we did a little carrier landing practice in San Diego Harbor. We were at what was called North Island. We did a few carrier landings and takeoffs. That in itself was a bit hairy. On landing, you came to a rather abrupt halt. There was a little bit of trauma. I never had to try it on the high seas. It was such a small landing surface, the pilot had to be really on the ball.

There were two guys on the tail of the carrier giving signals and stuff to the pilot. There were cables strung across the deck. When the hook under the plane grabbed, you got a jolt. About the time it came to a stop, the tail came up [as the nose dove forward]. It was a little hairy.

The pilot had arresting gear shoulder straps and a head strap. He had a high headrest, and he had a band across his forehead so his head couldn't snap forward.

As gunner, I faced aft. I had the support of the seat that way. The gunner had no high headrest, so we had to anticipate landing. During takeoff, the gunner sat facing forward. The catapult acceleration pushed you back into the seat. So, we did a few carrier takeoffs and landings right there in San Diego Harbor.

Then they sent us up to a place called Carney Mesa. I think it's called Lindbergh Field now, because that's where Colonel Lindbergh trained before he crossed the Atlantic Ocean. It was up in the hills about seventeen miles from San Diego. We didn't train too long there.

The SBD had dual controls [a second set of flight controls for the gunner]. I had to learn how to land the aircraft. They'd let us take over the controls and fly it. When I practiced landings, the pilot was following pretty closely on his controls. I could get it down if the pilot got shot.

According to Howard's history, the squadron shipped out of the States on 25 September 1943.

From there, we went to sea. I like to tell my friends that I went to sea on the Commodore Vanderbilt yacht, which is a fact. The commodore had a big seagoing yacht, a big steel ship he used to travel around the world. He gave it to the Navy at the start of World War II. They tore the superstructure off, moved the stacks from the center to the side, and put on a carrier deck. It was considerably shorter than the Forrestal class. Later in the war, they built what was called auxiliary aircraft carriers that were somewhat shorter. The commodore's ship was the *Nassau*, so the Navy named this the USS *Nassau*. The commodore had the courtesy to leave some of the printing establishment he had below deck. He had "shell back" cards there.

Shell back cards are issued to individuals who cross the equator and are properly initiated. Ships have shell back ceremonies such as plastering the candidate with eggs and hosing him off.

The commodore had prepared elaborate diploma-type plaques for his guests who joined the shell back club. We had our names printed on some of those, and I still have mine.

After a one-night liberty stop in Pearl Harbor—we could see the wreckage of the bombings—our first stop on the USS *Nassau* was Pago Pago, in American Samoa. It's a beautiful island with a magnificent harbor. At the head of the harbor is a huge volcanic peak. It had been inactive for many years, and the trees grow all the way up the sides. While we were there, we practiced takeoffs and landings on the

Nassau. We had some air-to-air training. Another airplane would pull a big wind sock, and we'd shoot at it with tracer bullets. We attacked a few little barges, probably garbage scows, trying to bomb and strafe them.

Howard notes the squadron moved to the French possession, Wallis Island, on 10 October 1943.

From Pago Pago, we were sent to Wallis Island, northeast of Samoa. There was a small French garrison there. The Frenchmen lived in privileged style. The war was on, but the French were not fighting the Japanese.

Next stop was Nukufetau in the southern part of the Ellice Islands. From there, we went up to another interesting island, Funafuti. That was in the heart of the Ellice Islands and was headquarters of the Fifth Fleet. Funafuti has a beautiful harbor.

The war department had decided to bypass the Marshall Islands, so our job was to keep the Japanese runways there out of service and to knock down the defenses. That was 1943. The Japanese fleet was gone, but the administrative headquarters was still there in a place called Jabortown on the island of Jaluit. There were substantial buildings there. A lot of the other islands had been occupied just for air bases. There were a few sunken ships in the harbors of some of the islands. We figured [whatever Japanese troops remained] were being supplied by submarine.

We spotted one Japanese submarine [probably attempting to resupply their troops],

and we tried to bomb it. It didn't take him long to dive. There were TBFs [torpedo bomber built by Grumman] in the theater [south pacific]. They could lay down torpedoes. I flew in TBFs a couple of times.

We had supporting fighter planes with us, F4Fs and F4Us. They went up after any Japanese planes that came our way, so the SBDs didn't encounter much air-to-air. We shot at a few [Japanese planes], but it wasn't the greatest threat. Most of the planes we lost were to ground fire. Flak makes a hell of a noise when it hits a metal airplane. It sounds like getting hit with a snow shovel. The SBD was a pretty tough plane—you'd see a plane coming in with metal flapping and pieces off.

The SBD wing had dive slabs. In the process of the dive, the pilot opened the flaps, which would slow our airspeed down. They acted like brakes. They had holes in them that would suck air and redirect it. Slowing the plane down gave the pilot more time to get on target.

Most of the time, we were not assigned a particular airplane, so the number of bombs painted on the nose of the aircraft indicated the number of bombing missions for that airplane.

A PBY went down near Nui island. We went up on patrol. A destroyer went in to pick up the downed crew.

We were working out of the Ellice Islands, Funafuti, and then Nukufetau doing mostly patrol work in the southern Gilberts. We moved up to Majuro, in the Marshalls where we were

to start daily bombing of the Jap-held islands Jaluit, Mille, Wotje, and Maloelap. Marine landing forces were taking Tarawa [an island on the north end of the Gilberts].

Five consecutive log entries cite missions searching for downed flights. Howard's notes for 4 March are: *The squadron attacked Jaluit Atoll carrying one-thousand-pound bombs each. Our target was heavy gun emplacements and the raid was very successful. Five SBDs were hit (none lost). By March 20, ten of the planes had received damage.*

A squadron of fighter planes that was supposed to be going to Nukufetau never made it there. We spent several days patrolling the area looking for them. They were all lost, probably a navigation error. I don't remember which type they were. We had two types of fighter planes: the F4U with the gull wings and the F4F *Hellcat* built by Grumman that looked like a big cigar. It didn't have much speed but was very maneuverable.

From Dick's log notes: *Escort USS* Independence *from Tarawa.* On 20 November 1943, the Marines landed on Tarawa.

Tarawa was not very far north of Funafuti. After Tarawa was taken, we landed there. The carnage was terrible. Bodies were everywhere. It was about four days after the last battle, and the bodies were really getting ripe. The Japanese were buried right there in big pits.

We flew missions in and out of Kwajalein and Eniwetok a few times. They were to the north and west of Tarawa, as was Bikini.

Log notes show bombing missions to Jaluit, Maloelap, Mille, and Wotje.

That's where Luke and Houston [two men in Dick's outfit] got shot down, over Maloelap, hit by flak. They went down in flames.

The gunner was expected to provide bomb damage information. He had a large, heavy Fairchild camera.

It was a big cumbersome thing. It looked like an oversized Speed Graphic, about one foot by one foot by one foot. It was arranged with trigger grip handles. We had to almost stand up, with the canopy opened, to put the camera over the side to get the pictures. You could feel the breeze, but it wasn't anything you couldn't resist. The camera wasn't mounted. We carried it aboard and picked it up when we needed it.

Another entry is *Cover life raft*.

A couple of our guys, Morgan and Joos, went down, so we covered them until they were picked up by a U.S. destroyer. That was kind of hairy. They went down near one of the islands and were drifting toward shore. The Japanese were firing at the life raft, while our squadron was strafing the shore. We had no bombs left at that point.

Other entries were: *Dropped message to DD* and *Pill boxes.*

On that one, we dropped a message to a destroyer. I don't know what it was about. The "pill boxes" were reinforced gun placements. Our primary mission was very accurate bombing. We'd knock out the pillboxes with one-thousand-pound bombs.

In April, Lieutenant Miller went down over Wotje and was forced to ditch. He and his gunner were picked up by a PBY.

On Majuro, we lived in tents, eight men to a tent. The mess hall was a tent set up with tables. We got a superabundance of mutton from Australia. It was the stringiest stuff. I liked lamb, but the stuff we got from Australia was not that great. And, of course, we got the usual stuff like "SOS" [shit on a shingle—military slang for chipped beef on toast], powdered eggs and powdered milk. They had refrigerators that ran on the generators. We'd get ice cream once in a while. One other treat we got was fresh fish. When they took garbage out into the lagoon, fish would come to feed. Somebody got the bright idea to get some fish. They took a couple of hand grenades out on the boat. They went out to a clear section of water and threw them over the side. When they detonated, the concussion killed a lot of fish. We'd skin and clean them up. The chef and his crew would cook them up for us. They got sick of doing that and discouraged us from fishing, but it did provide a little variety.

The urinal was a pipe driven into the coral with a funnel on top. The coral was pretty porous, so that's all there was to it. Time off included a few bottles of 3.2 beer, a weak brew. We drank that warm, and it had its effect out in the hot sun. You get used to warm beer. Most Europeans drink their beer warm. We enjoyed it. Another luxury the flight crews had was after each bombing mission, when we had our debriefing. They handed us a nip of Cornet brandy. The assumption being we were all shook up. The more enterprising gunners and pilots buddied up to the guys who didn't drink. They increased their ration that way.

The Seabees were very enterprising guys. They supplied us with a lot of good ideas. We'd catch water from the tent flies in fifty-gallon drums. They [the Seabees] showed us how to rig a shower with smaller tin cans tied up in a tripod to get them up above your head. One guy would dump water into the cans and let it trickle down as another guy lathered up.

Another Seabee innovation helped with a pest problem. The pests were mostly little lizards, harmless little critters. They didn't bother anyone except that occasionally, at night, one would crawl into bed with you, and it got squashed when you rolled over. We slept on canvas-and-wood cots. Along toward the later days, we did have rats that came ashore from the boats when they were unloading cargo. We used to have fun taking shots at them with our .38s [.38 caliber pistols]. After blackout conditions had been relaxed, we came up with the idea of eliminating rodents from the tents by putting a deck in the tent. We used half a dozen Marston mats [pierced metal planks between ten and twelve feet long and three feet wide]. We locked together several and pitched the tent over the mats. We had a line to the tent for the light bulb. We tapped into the electric source.

One of the guys had a wee bit of electrical experience. They had a gasoline generator somewhere on the island; there may have been more than one. The Seabees said we could split a wire, positive and negative, and tie one end to the Marston mats. Then, when we were all in bed at night, the last guy in the sack would connect the other wire. That gave the Marston mat a low-voltage current. That kept all the rodents out. That was okay unless someone forgot about it when he had to get up at night. It was low-voltage, so the shock was like that of a cattle fence.

The Seabees also made a washing machine of sorts. A propeller was attached to a horizontal crankshaft, and a vertical agitator was attached to the shaft. When the wind blew, which was most of the time, the propeller caused the agitator to work, helping to clean our clothes.

We had to use distilled water for drinking water—distilled from sea water, and it was always hot and not all that palatable: a necessity not a luxury. They had bags of water, like a goatskin bag, with a spigot near the bottom. Those bags may have been rubber or canvas. They'd be hung in strategic areas where you could get a drink. You'd use your canteen cup to pour yourself a slug of water.

Howard's notes: *May 14th started the squadron on*

night raids and twenty-hours-a-day attacks.

We had a mission nearly every day. Quite a bit of it was night flying. And quite of bit of it was in rainstorms.

One time, our target was some gun emplacements at the end of a runway. It was one of my last bombing missions over Mille Atoll. We had overshot the target, so the pilot reversed his direction, which meant, to get on target, we had to finish up flying directly down the Japanese runway. We got plastered with shells, a lot of flak. We tried to avoid reversing directions. I had sort of a fatalistic attitude even though I knew there was some chance I wouldn't come back. That was up until that last bombing mission.

My total tour was sixteen months. I left the Pacific before VE [Victory in Europe] Day. The battles for Saipan and Tinian had been won. The Marines were there. The end of the war was in sight.

The conquest of Saipan was declared complete 9 July 1944. Germany surrendered unconditionally 7 May 1945.

About the time I finished my tour, the Marines were replacing the SBD with a new dive bomber built by Curtiss, the SBD2C. There weren't too many SBDs left. The SBD2C was called the *Helldiver*. It was a lousy airplane. It was big, and it wasn't maneuverable. The pilots didn't like it. I think it had twin fifties in place of the thirty cals.

The war was winding down.

Our SBDs were given to another squadron at Eniwetok, and our squadron started to retrain in SBD2Cs. It was at that point that we were sent back to the States.

One of my favorite stories has to do with coming back from overseas. When we went over, we carried our dress uniforms in a sea bag. At various locations, we encountered dampness and, of course, dampness does a job on leather. So, most of us had thrown away our dress shoes long before we came back. Occasionally, we'd air out our dress greens on a clothesline. The result was a bleached lighter color of green—what we called "the salty look," like old salts.

We came back on the aircraft carrier, USS *Hollandia*. From Majuro, we sailed to Ford Island. That's in the main harbor of Oahu, Pearl Harbor. The guys were anticipating our first liberty in the States [military personnel were required to wear their uniform at all times]. Nobody had dress shoes. Somebody got the bright idea of going to the Navy ship's store. Navy shoes were identical to ours, except ours were cordovan brown and the Navy shoes were black. We thought we might get away with black shoes. Guys spent time on shipboard from Hawaii to the States polishing those shoes to a high gloss.

On our first liberty in San Diego, a bunch of us went down looking for girls. We ended up in the village of Linda Vista at night. One of the guys, Nick, was hitting it off with a girl. Finally, we said it was time to go back. We had to stand muster in the morning. He said, "I'll see you guys. Take off."

The next morning, we had muster. The sergeant or officer was calling off names. We knew Nick was missing. The word had gone out that he wasn't there for muster. When he called Nick's name, about ten guys yelled, "Here." The guy calling roll decided to let it go. He pretended he didn't hear. A few minutes went by, and there was tittering in the rear ranks. Nick was coming across the drill field. The laughs got riotous when somebody looked down and instead of his brand new Navy shoes, he was wearing a pair of pebble-grained, wing-toed, civilian shoes. I sometimes think of war in terms of the good times we had.

I was back in the States in January of 1945. While we were in San Diego, part of our group was sent to Tsingtao, China. They were to transport captured Japanese officers back. There was still some military action going on over there. Our guys were to support the transport planes.

I was only at San Diego for a short while. They sent me back to the east coast, to Oak Grove, North Carolina. I was supposed to teach gunnery, but the war was winding down, and I was largely waiting for my discharge. They had introduced a point system, which I was well qualified for. You got points for being overseas and points for missions. Anyway, I had more than enough points

for discharge. As a matter of fact, I had enough points when we were in the islands. Supposedly, when you got enough points, you could get out, but they didn't observe the rules too carefully. If they needed you, you stayed.

So I putzed around North Carolina for awhile teaching gunnery, antiaircraft gunnery which I had no prior experience at. They asked me at that point if I wanted to go to officers training school, but I opted not to. I was discharged there in North Carolina. I had forty-three combat missions and 516 flying hours. The last log entry is 5 May 1945. I didn't get home until after the fall semester at University of New Hampshire had started in 1945. I did get home for Christmas.

George F. Fiske, Jr., Of Athol — United States Navy, 1943-1945

On Patrol Near Iwo And Okinawa Shores

GEORGE FISKE found himself in Japan in 1945. On the way, he met action in the Pacific.

When the Japanese attacked Pearl Harbor, George Fiske was in high school in Fitchburg.

I was visiting friends on School Street in Athol, Massachusetts, opposite the middle school. We had been to Packard Heights ice skating. If you were going into the military, you could graduate after finishing half of your senior year—provided your grades were okay. I enlisted in the Navy in October of 1943, and was called to duty on February 4, 1944. My Dad had been in the Navy in World War I.

First stop was basic training at Samson, New York, on the shore of Lake Geneva.

Bob Truehart from Athol was there as was Doctor [Duane] Talcott [an Athol dentist]. I had a tooth problem. When they examined it, I mentioned I knew Commander Talcott, so they called him in. He looked at it and told the ensign to fill the tooth, and I still have it today. I remember Bob because, after the war, when I came to Athol to start this business [Fiske Funeral Home], I spotted him. He looked familiar. We had a lot to talk about. I hadn't seen him since boot camp. Boot camp was four or five weeks nothing special. Except it was COLD. That was February in upper New York state.

Warmer climes called. Out of boot camp, George

was first assigned to Jacksonville, Florida, the naval air station used for aviation training. He was supposed to become a radio operator in various Navy aircraft.

After some ground school, we went up in *PBY*s. I also got a ride in a dive bomber. I wasn't that good at code; I had to write it on my knee pad or try to remember it. We got some radar training as well as radio. In the dive bombers, I really didn't like going down in that steep dive. I was sitting backwards. They put gun sights from the planes on shotguns, and we shot skeet. Then, we'd shoot with some guns without the sights, just to learn to lead the target. Anyway, I requested sea duty.

George didn't finish the radio or radar schools, but he did get enough to put his talents to use later. He got his wish for sea duty through orders to Charleston, South Carolina, a receiving station, and was assigned to Fort Pierce, Florida, for amphibious training. Another sailor who had opted out of aviation and accompanied George to Fort Pierce, volunteered for Scouts and Raiders (small commando units). George and the other sailor would meet again in Okinawa.

We had a choice of type of ships. I said "What's the biggest you have?" The new LCS[L] [Landing Craft Support (Large)] was it. They as-

signed me to the LCS[L] training unit. An LCS[L] was a new gun boat. It was 158 feet long, had a twenty-three-foot eight-inch beam, a draft of five feet, eight inches, and displaced 381 tons. Her complement was eight officers and seventy men.

> **An LCS(L) was a new gun boat. It was 158 feet long, had a twenty-three-foot eight-inch beam, a draft of five feet, eight inches, and displaced 381 tons. The armament was two twin forty-millimeter guns, one single forty-millimeter, four single twenty-millimeter, and ten rocket launchers. The rest of the ship was ammo.**

The armament was two twin forty-millimeter guns, one single forty-millimeter, four single twenty-millimeter, and ten rocket launchers. The rest of the ship was ammo. I never thought much about that until we had to unload all of the rocket ammunition one night. That's a lot of ammunition. The ship didn't have a *V* hull to cut through the water, but it had a kettle bottom, sort of rounded. It really rode up over the waves and crashed down on the other side, a very rough ride. Our mission was to set up a picket line to protect other ships and forces. It was very slow, but it was good for what they used it for. Usually, there would be two or three LCSs with one destroyer plus air cover. The seventy-eight men on an LCS[L] were all types needed to run a ship: gunners, cooks, machinist, seamen, pharmacist. Everybody aboard ship had training on the guns. Everyone could

fire.

There weren't any training ships available or mockups at the base in Florida. Orders for more schooling sent George and the new gun ship crews to Solomons, Maryland (a point in the southern part of Maryland that juts into the Chesapeake Bay). Gunnery started with three-inch guns. Then they moved up to twenty-millimeter and forty-millimeter. Targets were set up on remote islands in the bay. They trained as a crew.

We fired the twenties at the range at some targets they had set up. They had one LCS[L]. I think it may have been Number 1.

Then they moved on to Bremerton, Washington, to pick up the brand new craft.

We went by train—cattle car as I remember it—to Bremerton. The ship wasn't quite ready, so we stayed at some barracks in Portland, Oregon, for a week or two. Only about 146 were built; ours was Number 64.

Souvenirs from Portland, Oregon, in George's scrapbook indicate the stay there. Then the LCS(L) went on to San Diego for final fitting, crew adjustments, and rendezvous for the Pacific crossing. Says the ship's history, ...*when the crew was battle ready (they) moved west to Pearl Harbor, arriving on 20 Feb-*

ruary 1945. She was placed in LCS(L)Group Eleven of LCS(L) Flotilla Four. She stopped at Eniwetok on 9 March and at Saipan on 18 March before departing with an invasion force for the Okinawa invasion on 25 March 1945.

We weren't in a convoy, just a group of LCS[L]s. We went to Hawaii, then to Eniwetok, then to Saipan; it had recently been taken. On one trip, near Wake island, we hit a typhoon. We didn't lose anyone, but just trying to get there was memorable. We had a good skipper, a lieutenant. Most of our officers were pretty good. The engineering officer was a mustang [came through the enlisted ranks before being commissioned]. We were headed for the invasion of Okinawa.

Navy historian Samuel Eliot Morison, in *History of United States Naval Operations*, reports the new LCS(L)s in action at Iwo Jima 19 February 1945. Morison reports four of them fighting fires on the LST *884* after it was damaged by a Japanese *kamikaze* plane. Armand Dugas, who would be fire chief in Athol, was aboard the *884* and tells of his view elsewhere in this volume. From George Fiske's LCS(L) history: *As the Naval gunfire barrage lifted off the beaches on 1 April 1945, Easter Sunday morning, the assault waves moved forward accompanied by the LCS(L) 64 which provided close inshore gunfire support. However, when the landing craft were within a few yards of Sakibaru Saki, they turned and returned to sea. The operation was only a feint to draw some of the enemy away from the true invasion area.*

I was part of that feint. We went in on the southeastern side of the island. [The invasion would take place on the west side]. We went in there, and I couldn't see anything. All I saw was a horse. We fired for a while and then came out, and that was it. We were just trying to get them to split their forces.

Following the establishment and expansion of the beachhead, the battle for the island shifted to the air as the Japanese launched their suicide planes. The U.S. Navy plan called for placing picket stations around the island to warn the main fleet of incoming *kamikazes*. LCS(L) Flotilla Four was designated a radar picket support craft unit. One or two LCS(L)s were assigned to each larger ship, and they remained on station for ten days. After ten days, they returned to Hagushi Anchorage for four days to get provisions and ammo. Hagushi is on the west side of Okinawa where the first attack was made and was one of the first areas secured. At 0400 on 3 April 1945, the LCS(L) *64* splashed—military slang for *shot down*—one enemy aircraft (confirmed by the USS Prichett (DD 561).

There were plenty of *kamikazes*. We shot one down the first night. Later, we shot down another near Keise Shima [an island west of Okinawa]. We were part of that attack. That's where Ernie Pyle, the Pulitzer Prize war correspondent, got killed. The rest of the time we did picket duty, patrolling an area to keep the Japanese one- and two-man subs away from the fleet. Those subs were really just manned torpedoes. We could stay out about a week or ten days. Then we went in for supplies. At night, we couldn't stay at anchorage because of those suicide subs, so we cruised all night. We called that skunk patrol. We spent the night looking for periscopes.

Only one officer did not impress George, the navigation officer. On night picket, he said he didn't need the help of the radar man.

We were on one of those skunk patrols. He ran us right up on the beach. The guy driving the ship had decided he didn't need radar. The captain wasn't too happy. He was already in his bunk. Fortunately, we had a good engineering officer. We got the screws pulling backwards and got us off, but we were exposed for quite a while. We were south of Naha, and that hadn't been secured yet. Some were ready to abandon ship, but the engineering officer stayed calm.

On Day 6 of the Okinawa invasion, George met his old friend from Fort Pierce—the one who had joined a small commando unit.

After several days, I was coming down a ladder on an LST supply ship. My friend was lying there, his arm in a sling. I asked what had happened. He said he ended up on a submarine. He had been put ashore on the island of Okinawa at night about six days *before* the invasion and had been on the island ever since. He was the radio man for that advance party. All of the men in that unit were trained in underwater demolition or were Marines.

The ground battle for Okinawa got tougher and messier. Naval forces controlled the seas except for continuing *kamikaze* attacks and worry about one- and two-man suicide submarines.

We did picket duty day and night. On one of the resupplies, we tied up to the battleship USS *New Mexico*, an old World War I ship. It was an experience for me, because my father had served on the *New Mexico*.

During the *kamikaze* attack when the *64* got its second kill, the USS *Bush* got hit by two *kamikazes*. At least ninety-five men from the *Bush* were pulled aboard the LCS(L) *64* before she headed back toward the anchorage.

Our first real experience of the war was with the *Bush*. She

had been hit by a *kamikaze*, and we tied up to her to take off the wounded. There were wounded all over the forward deck. We were still under attack, and we were ordered to chop our lines. We were only a little way away when it got hit again on the other side of the bow. It blew the wounded into the water. We spent the rest of the time, all that night, picking up men from the water.

Our skipper was clever. The rockets we carried came in tubes with a screw on top. Empty with the top screwed on, they made excellent flotation devices, so he ordered us to jettison the rockets and throw the cases overboard. Many of those guys were hanging onto rocket cases when we pulled them aboard. I thought he should have gotten a medal for that idea. The captain of the *Bush* outranked our captain, so the minute he came aboard, he took control. We knew he had taken over, because [unlike George's captain] this fellow went zigzag like a destroyer. We brought all those guys—there must have been nearly a hundred—to the anchorage.

Many years later, I met a man in my funeral home who had been in the Navy. As we talked, he said he was on a destroyer. When I asked which one, he said, "the Bush." He had been pulled out of the water by the crew of an LCS[L]. We've been friends ever since. The *Bush* survivors have a convention each year, and I've been invited.

We had one close call with a *kamikaze*. There were several up there. One wiggled his wings, peeled off, and came at us. Coming in, he lowered his

landing gear to create maximum impact. We were shooting, and he hit just short, about thirty yards away. That was our closest call to being hit.

From Okinawa, the LCS(L) sailed for Leyte Gulf in the Philippines. The ship's history says, *By 10 July 1945, the island had been secured and the* kamikaze *attacks broken. That day the LCS(L) 64 with the majority of the LCS(L) Flotilla Four departed from Okinawa for Tacloban, Leyte, Philippine Islands.* They were destined to be a part of the giant armada being formed for the invasion of the Japanese mainland.

That's where I got sick—amoebic dysentery. Apparently, one of the cruisers got a load of bad water. They passed it to us during resupply. The Japanese didn't know it, but the percentage of the forces in the Philippines who were very sick was high. I ended up on the USS *Relief*, a hospital ship very appropriately named for patients with dysentery. I lost nearly fifty pounds. I almost died.

Finally well enough to return to work, a thinner George Fiske rejoined the ship in the Leyte Gulf, where he was when A-bombs were dropped on Hiroshima and Nagasaki.

The whole Leyte Gulf was covered with ships. All of them were firing. From there, we took troops up to Tokyo and were there for security.

Departing from Japan on

George's bout with dysentery left him rail thin, above. He was sent back to duty and then to a hospital.

3 December 1945, the LCS(L) *64* stopped at Pearl Harbor before continuing to the Panama Canal and Green Cove Springs, Florida, where she was decommissioned.

From there, we went to the Panama Canal and up to New Orleans. I entered the hospital there, and the ship went on to Green Cove Springs to be mothballed.I stayed in the hospital in New Orleans until I got discharged. Then I took advantage of the GI Bill. That's how I got into this business.

On 28 February 1949, her designation was changed from LCS(L) *64* to LSSL *64*, [Landing Ship Support, Large]. Under the Mutual Defense Assistance Program, the LSSL *64* was transferred to the Republic of Italy in July 1951 and renamed *Molosso*.

I heard that a few years later they sold the ship to the Italian Navy. They renamed it an Italian name for watchdog. Later, through a ham radio friend, I learned it was taken to a junk yard for scrap. The only LCS[L] that I know of that is still afloat is over in Bangkok.

In August, 1994, George spent five days at the LCS(L) fiftieth anniversary reunion. Some nine hundred husbands and wives attended, but only two of George's shipmates.

Leona Cloutier Of Orange   **United States Navy, 1942-1946; 1948-1959**

Administrative Wizardry: "Be On Time"

A little less tall than the rest of the brass at Keyport, Washington, Lieutenant Commander LEONA CLOUTIER was head-and-shoulders above most personnel as chief administrative officer. She eventually served in the Pentagon with Admiral Arleigh Burke as her immediate supervisor.

Leona Cloutier loves people. She's a self-organized hard worker—an ideal candidate for the first group of women who formed the Woman Accepted for Volunteer Emergency Service (WAVES), the female force of the United States Navy. When World War II started, she had experience needed by the Navy, but the WAVES wouldn't be formed until 1948. Before going to the Dennison Manufacturing Company in Framingham, Massachusetts, Leona had worked for the Commonwealth of Massachusetts Department of Corrections in the women's reformatory at Framingham. There, she learned how to take fingerprints. Industries like Dennison had to be sure the employees had their fingerprints taken before they could do government work. Fingerprinting was typical of all industries with government projects. While working at Dennison in the personnel office, Leona became active with the Framingham Civil Defense Committee.

I offered my time nights to go into the factory to fingerprint the employees. That was when I first became very interested in helping in what was the oncoming war. That was 1943. Actually, I enlisted in December of 1942.

Leona first took a test to enter the Army reserve. She passed and would have been accepted, but she didn't "measure up" to the Army's minimum height of five feet, five inches for members of the first group selected to be ordered to active duty. She then applied for the Navy reserves and, in November of 1942, was accepted and enlisted formally 22 December 1942. When spaces were available (13 February 1943), she was ordered to active duty to the officer training course at Smith College, Northampton, Massachusetts. There she learned about Navy customs and traditions.

They didn't take me then because they didn't have the space to train us. And I was not sent down to Smith College, where I was to be trained after I enlisted in November of 1942. I didn't go on active until the

> **I enlisted in November of 1942. I didn't go on active until the 13th of February of 1943. During training we learned about what we might have to do, how hard we would have to work, that we would always be bossed by somebody, and to do our best.**

thirteenth of February of 1943. During training we learned about what we might have to do, how hard we would have to work, that we would always be bossed by somebody, and to do our best.

The Navy was an organization of orders. We learned we'd have to titivate [to keep clean] our spaces and to teach others to titivate their spaces. We had to do a lot of physical exercises. We marched three times a day from Smith College to downtown Northampton for our meals.

It was very cold that winter. One of the girls who came from Florida just about froze to death. We were told never to talk in line and never to talk unless spoken to. We went on a trip to Filene's to get our clothing. They didn't have a coat that would fit me because I was so short. On our way back, the driver took the wrong road out of Northampton. Because I

knew the area, I knew we were going the wrong way, but I didn't say anything. After we were lost for about an hour, we stopped at a gas station and found out we had to go back. In the meantime, the people at the college were looking for us. Everything in the military runs on a schedule. After, someone said to me "Didn't you know where you were going? You're a Massachusetts girl."

I said "Yes, I did, but I was told 'No talking,' so I didn't say a word."

As administrative officers, some were sent to additional schools like accounting. Six of us were sent for administration, and we didn't get very much instruction except "use good judgment." Most didn't have much prior administrative experience, except the college presidents and people like that, and they were lecturing and selecting the women for the service. I was older, thirty-three years old.

The Smith course lasted from the thirteenth of February to the sixth of April. After training, I became an Ensign in the U.S. Naval Reserve on the sixth of April 1943.

Ms. Cloutier was assigned to the commandant of the First Naval District—the head Navy man in the area.

When I went to report to him, his assistant said he was sorry that they didn't have any place in the office for a woman. I was told to come in the next morning and talk to the personnel officer. He was a retired personnel captain who had come on active duty. I went to see

On Duty...
Geography
Leona Cloutier

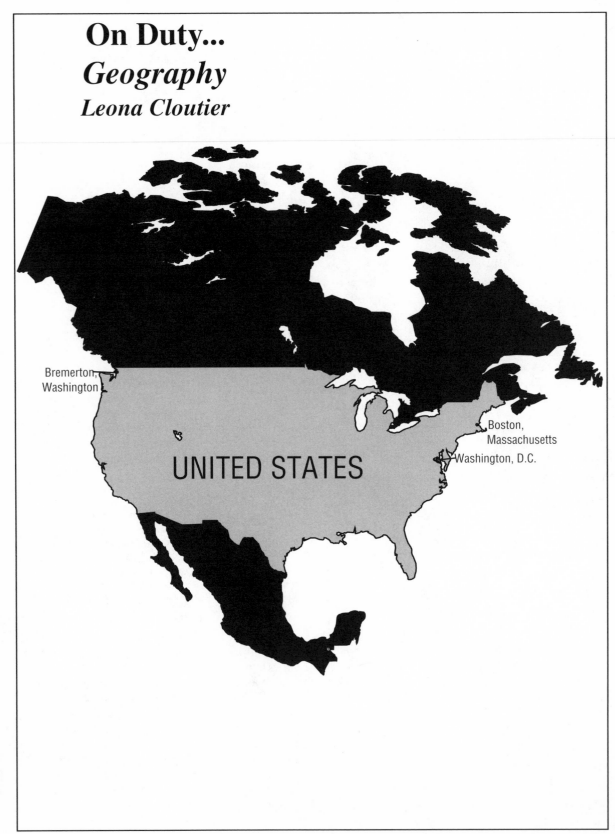

him, and he handed me a list of job descriptions. I did not know what most of them meant.

I saw something that said "family allowance division" and one that said Insurance, but most of the activities didn't mean much to me. I was trying to relate my background to the duties. The captain said they were all new departments, and I would be setting them up. Since I had worked in personnel and had a background in people and problems, I took the family allowance division.

"Family allowance" in the Navy was a big job. Most of the men who came into the Navy had not taken out any insurance. Legislation had passed that they would automatically get government insurance, so we had to find who should be their beneficiaries. The men had left families at home without any money, and finding who should be their beneficiaries was my responsibility. We were constantly setting up allowances for families under set conditions. Allowances were taken out of the pay. Laws were being made as we went along.

Without warning, Leona's duties suddenly changed. The government had created a traveling show to generate support for the war effort and for the sale of War Bonds. Leona was called into an office where she was told she was going to go out with the young women who were going to be in the war bond show.

Immediately, I got called

away from the job I was doing. I turned over my personnel division to a man who had been in the office for a while and went out on this trip for a month. None of the enlisted women I had [in the show troupe] were from my organization. I had responsibility for all the female entertainers. I didn't even know them. They came from the Coast Guard, Navy, Army, and Army Air Corps to form the Department of Massachusetts War Bond group. The show was called "Direct Hit."

I asked for a place to have all of these women together so I could let them know who I was and what I expected. The War Bond group got me into Fenway Park in Boston. I said "I can see you are all handsome people, and all clean, and I know you're all talented, so I can't sell you anything. I'm just going to be your grandmother for a while." There I was at thirty one and these kids were from eighteen to twenty-one. I said, "I'm not going to teach you a thing. You know what you have to do and how to do it, but you have to do it ON TIME."

We went to twenty-eight cities. We put on shows, parts of shows, whatever we could do to entertain people. The show included two guests, Veronica Lake and Jack Dempsey. Jack Dempsey would go with the men, and Veronica Lake would go with the women. We traveled by bus. Each girl had to have her clothing for the month, so there weren't as many people as would normally fit into a bus, because of the extra clothing.

I was responsible for ten bus

loads of ladies. Marines went ahead to set up the shows and check for security, and the huge Coast Guard band traveled with us. All the people of importance in a town—selectmen and mayors—were so anxious to sell bonds that they had created all kinds of places for us to go. Perhaps five of my ladies would go and sing to the ladies' circle [woman's club]. When we got into a place like Boston, the whole show was put on, but in smaller towns, we'd do several smaller shows. The big shows were such a big hit, all the littler places wanted a part of it.

We all worked morning until night, and I mean we worked. We slept in YMCAs, YWCAs, and private homes. I stayed in one private home that was owned by the owner of a company and, my gracious! They treated me like I was the Queen of England.

Each place we went, the people who had invited us were responsible for feeding the troupe. We ate in restaurants, Legion halls, K of Cs. The associations in the towns were dying to get us. My only requirement was that they be on time, ON TIME. I told my girls, if they got delayed, not to be rude, but to just smile and say, "We'll see you later."

It was hit and run, work hard, day and night. We started with breakfast about six-thirty. We'd get on the bus and drive to get at our first stop at eight or nine o'clock in the morning and immediately start putting on [smaller] shows. In the evening, we'd really get busy putting on bigger shows. Some of the local people would talk about buying bonds. The show people didn't sell bonds. I was never asked to sell a bond; I had all I could do to take care of my girls.

Some days, I couldn't get what we needed, like shoes. The performers had no time to go and shop. Usually, I could get what we needed. I'd take one of the worn-out shoes to a local store and try to get another pair, but sometimes I couldn't because I didn't have the ration stamps.

Occasionally, we could get into the YWCA with a little extra time so the girls could take baths or a swim. I treated the girls like part of my family. They needn't look at my stripe. I was the head of the family. If they had any trouble, they were to come to Grandmother. They were wonderful.

Jack Dempsey and Veronica Lake were the salespeople for the bonds. They talked to the audience about buying bonds. Veronica Lake could get the whole crowd crying. Jack Dempsey told them it was their job to "fight for the country" by buying bonds. Tables were set up on the sides where local bankers sold the bonds.

It's unbelievable as I look back on it, because I never had time to think. I wasn't sure from one day to another if we'd have clothes enough and how we could keep going. The show had been written and practiced to perfection. Every one of the men and women who were in the show were quality people. They could have gone to any show or been in the movies.

The bond drive generated nine million dollars in sales.

That was a record, and Leona received a citation for her efforts. At the end of the exhausting tour a month later, she went back to the family allowance division at the First Naval District. She finished organizing that office. That task accomplished, she was assigned to Great Lakes, Illinois, to teach civilian readjustment, a new discharge briefing. The briefing was designed to reorient Navy personnel back into civilian society.

They sent me for one week of training at the Navy personnel office in Washington. I taught the personnel people who would be processing the men and women who would be getting out. My people would be telling them what their entitlements were.

That lasted sixty days, and then she was discharged on 12 January, 1946, Leona returned to her job at Dennison. When the opportunity to become part of the regular Navy finally came, Leona was ready. In 1948, Congress passed a law creating the WAVES. Lieutenant Leona was one of the first 288 in the country selected for commission in the regular Navy under the provisions of the Woman's Armed Services Integration Act of 1948. She was one of only two selected from the inactive reserves.

At Dennison, they were very good to me. They had raised my pay and benefits and were just very good to me. My mother was eighty-four years old, and she said, "Leona, you loved the Navy, and I loved having you there. You were so happy. Why don't you go back in?" I told her about the regular Navy and that I'd have to make out an application.

Between my mother and the good people at Dennison, they convinced me to take the test for the regular Navy. So, I did, and I was very, very proud to be selected. I was one of thirty-two New England woman first selected for the regular Navy. I went back in on the first of December, 1948. In order to be eligible for regular Navy, you had to pass the test. And if you were selected, you could remain in the service if you were promoted regularly to the rank of lieutenant commander before age forty. If you didn't get promoted, you were sent home [discharged].

Her first assignment in the regular Navy was at the naval receiving station in Norfolk, Virginia. She was the personnel officer there. After two years, she was promoted from personnel to the administrative officer. In the military, there is always a higher command structure, but Leona was the chief administrative officer for the base.

I did all kinds of things. Legal—whatever the job required. One thing made me very proud. I received a group of enlisted women out of training at Great Lakes. It was the first time the Navy allowed men and women to train together. It worked out beautifully. I had the supervision responsibility of the five hundred women. The men and women got along well. I didn't use the fact that I was a lieutenant, because I knew that they did the work and that they should get the credit for it. I was very happy with that job.

She left there in February, 1952, for Quonset Naval Air Station in Rhode Island. Personnel work on an air station was different.

I recognized the flyers by the shoes. The regular Navy personnel wear black shoes, but the regular air Navy wears brown shoes. So I referred to them as black shoe or brown shoe. I was both the personnel officer and administrative officer for the base.

The aircraft carrier USS *Bennington*, on maneuvers off the New England coast had a boiler blow up. It was on a holiday. Injuries were many, and confusion reigned.

The *Bennington* had picked up reserves at Quonset Point, as they had at other stations, for training. It was just before Memorial Day. There were seven thousand men on board. I was responsible for the records of all the enlisted men. On the morning of Memorial Day, at five o'clock, on the phone I heard "Leona, get to your desk; there is an emergency."

Dispatches were coming in. Some were for the medics, and some for other parts of the Navy. We didn't know what the situation was. It was the holiday weekend, and I only had three yeomen [office personnel] available. I called Newport and got three more men to help. I knew we'd need uniforms to dress the deceased before we sent them home. I could cut orders to have uniforms issued, but the clothing section was closed for the holiday. I called the clothing officer and asked that the supply section be open. Part of my job was to arrange to send the bodies home. People were coming in and calling in like mad. We needed a place for the dependents of the men on board to wait, so we turned the gym over to them.

I realized the first thing the men on the ship would want was to let the folks know. NBC had already arrived, and the story of the accident was on the air. I talked with the communication officer, who agreed to set something up right where the ship docked. Each man got to send a one-line: "I'm okay, letter-to-follow" to their next of kin or loved one. I arranged for ambulances. The hospitals were loaded. Several hundred were injured.

I had no records on many of the men. I called the naval department for records, because I had to write orders to transfer men to hospitals or send the deceased home. When the records section couldn't provide order numbers, I decided to use my own system: One, Two, Three, Four...

I had worked three days and three nights without sleep. When they said I should attend a memorial Mass on the ship, I said, "Sir, I will not be there. I need some sleep." I was a wreck, and I was a mess. My clothes were dirty. I'd be embarrassed, so I didn't attend.

Four days later, the captain picked up copies of all my orders and flew with me into Washington to the Bureau of Naval Personnel. He said, "Tell them what you want." I gave them the orders numbered from one to seventy-two. I said I had done the best I could, and I didn't want to ever be asked any questions about the orders.

At that time, I didn't know how many had lost their lives. In November of 1954, when Archbishop Richard Cushing came to say a memorial Mass for the one hundred and three men who had lost their lives, I found out how many had died.

The dead included the ship's personnel officer and one of the *Blue Angel* pilots. I was at a party at the O Club with the *Blue Angels* the night before they shipped out on that training trip.

One of my toughest decisions was where to send one of the bodies. The parents were separated, and both wanted their son's remains. I found out that the man had always gone to his mother's house when on leave, so that's how I made the decision.

As a result of her work during the *Bennington* accident, Leona was given an exceptional assignment. That exceptional assignment was to the torpedo station at Keyport, Washington, near Puget Sound.

The Navy people at Quonset Point Naval Air Station didn't know the assignment was exceptional. And nobody could tell me what the assignment was. To try to help me find out about this new job, the public relations officer at Quonset Point wrote to the station at Keyport and asked them what they did. When the letter arrived at Keyport, I was confronted with people who came to ask a lot of questions like why I wanted to know what they did out there. I was told it was a classified station, and I would not be told what it was or what goes on out there.

The interviewers said it was a beautiful station and I would love it. They [FBI and Navy security people] took down all my history, called captains and people I had worked with, and tried to find if anybody had anything on me. The interview lasted for two days.

Cleared by the security search, Leona drove across the country. Her sister-in-law joined her in the cross-country trek and continued to California to visit family there.

When we got to Bremerton, Washington, I stopped at the big Navy base there and asked about Keyport. They told me it was twenty miles away. We went to the housing office to ask about rentals, because I thought I'd have to live in Bremerton and commute to Keyport. They told me I would get housing at Keyport, and we could stay in a "religious room" [the Navy held open two or three rooms for the chaplains who were in transit to and from ships]. They let us stay there because it was during the week. We arrived on a Monday morning.

We went to get some food. While shopping I heard, "Will the person with the Massachusetts license plate come to the desk immediately?"

I went up, and the gentlemen there said, "Do you drive an Oldsmobile?"

I said "Yes."

He said, "I have just demolished your car."

He had backed into my car with a great big truck loaded with fruit. Well, I didn't know whether to cry or what. I was in civilian clothes. When I told him I was a Navy officer on my way to a new job, and I hadn't even reported in yet, he said, "What kind of a car do you want?" He admitted he was completely at fault, and within three hours, replaced my car with a brand new Oldsmobile just like the one he had ruined.

The next day, Leona went to Keyport to report. The station was close enough to the ocean so, when you were up on the hills, you could see torpedoes being tested in the water. The operations at the base were highly classified.

The operations at the station were so classified that in 1985, when I went West, I wanted to see where I had lived, but they still wouldn't let me in. When reporting for duty at Keyport, I was met at the gate and taken to the commanding officer. He welcomed me and asked me if I wanted my house painted. I said I didn't have a house. He said I was the only woman on the station and, as administrative officer, I was to have a house. The house had six rooms and a gar-

den. It was beautiful. I said I didn't need that much house, and I was sure there were officers with children who needed a bigger house. When I asked for a smaller house, the captain said, "Who ever heard of such a thing?" But he gave me a wonderful four-room house up on the hill.

There were numerous women in the civilian work force at the station, but Leona was the only female military person. Her responsibilities included personnel and administrative duties for all military, Navy and Marine.

I had several chiefs working for me, and there is no one better than a good chief in the Navy. I had a bunch of chiefs who had never been through high school. I got them together and told them we were going to get them their high school diplomas. I knew they would need a high school education when they got out. Most of them were technical workers, and they had good heads. They needed the academics, so we worked on the Graduate Equivalent Diploma [GED]. When the officer in charge of the Marines left, they moved me down to that house, closer to the "big wigs." I loved that little house up on the hill. I loved Keyport.

One day, while she was sitting at her desk, one of the chiefs came in with a long letter from the Pentagon. Leona had been reassigned to the Office of the Chief of Naval Operations at the Pentagon.

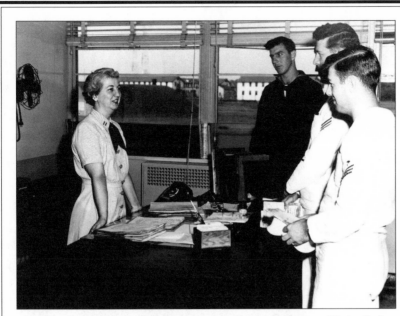

In her office with members of her staff, Leona took pride in their excellent teamwork and accomplishments. "There is no one better than a good chief in the Navy," she said. With her help, those who hadn't been to high school earned Graduate Equivalency Diplomas (GEDs).

She loved the Keyport assignment and the area, but this was a "prestige" move, not to be refused.

I started to cry. The one thing I didn't want to do was go to Washington, D.C. I didn't have the experience to be in Washington; that's where things come from. Well, my captain didn't want me to leave, so he went with me to Washington and spoke up for me. He said "She's doing a wonderful job for us, keeps her mouth shut, does everything possible in the administrative job, and we just can't spare her".

They said, "Do you want to see her desk?"

I was to have twenty-three people working for me, responsible for all the of the civilian workers as well as the enlisted personnel over at the receiving station as well as those that were in the office of the Chief of Naval Operations—twenty-three hundred people in all. So we went back to Keyport until the orders came in. I made LCDR, USN [Lieutenant Commander] while at Keyport.

The Keyport assignment was from 31 August 1954, until 16 April 1956. With the new promotion, Leona knew she could stay in the Navy until retirement (military policy required officers to make promotions within certain "time-in-grade"). She served at the Pentagon from 17 May 1956 until her retirement 29 February 1959.

Arleigh Burke [Admiral Burke, Chief of Naval Operations] was my boss. He later served on the Joint Chiefs of Staff.

Leona is especially proud of a citation from Admiral Burke. It cited several of her accomplishments, notably her handling of the *Bennington* disaster.

Admiral Burke called me in when he realized I'd have to retire. [Military rules specified age/rank requirements. Leona entered the service later than most and got caught by that prohibition]. He said "Leona, the next selection is only three months away. Let's make out a letter saying you're especially needed for those three months." I said I had come in under the law, and I would go out under the law. I had people to take care of, and I knew I could get a civilian job. I thought if I made the promotion, I would serve another five years. I could get a civilian job at age fifty better than I could at age fifty-five. So I retired.

Leona had really grown to like Washington, D. C. She was offered, and accepted, the position of administrative vice-president for the Washington office of the Philco Corporation. Three years later, when Ford bought Philco, she was offered the personnel job at Ford but turned it down because it would require her to move out of Washington. After some public relations work, she went to the Virginia Employment Commission where she stayed until she again retired in 1959.

Arthur P. "Art" Tarolli of Athol　　　　**United States Army, 1951-1953**

Silver Star Service During A Strange War

On 25 June 1950, the newspapers reported the United Nations rebuke of the North Koreans for their attack on South Korea. On 27 June, the UN and the United States agreed to send troops to aid Seoul. On 31 July, President Harry S. Truman ordered the mobilization of National Guard troops and a Selective Service draft of one hundred thousand men.

By late July, the North Koreans had pushed the South Korean forces into a small pocket in the southeast corner of their country. On 9 November 1950, the Chinese entered the Korean conflict. It was these Chinese troops that Arthur would face. On 26 July 1951, North and South Korea agreed to start peace talks, but the war was still going on and men were still being drafted. Arthur Tarolli was one of them.

After I got out of high school, I went to work at Eastern Furniture. My father and mother worked there. I probably would have stayed there until the place closed because I hadn't gone to college. I was working there comfortably. I got out of high school in 1947. I worked at Eastern Furniture until 1951. I left there because, like a lot of other guys, I got

drafted. I went into the service in September of 1951. The local draft board included Libby Cooke and Johnny Johnstone. Jim Cetto and I hung around together. On our high school baseball team, I was the pitcher, and he was the catcher. I went in with Jim Cetto, Joe Musante, and "Koko" Koroblis. Koko was six- four or -five. He was a basketball player—a good-looking guy. We were all basically going into the Army, but if the Marine Corps saw somebody they thought was pretty good, they'd tap him. Koroblis ended up in the Marine Corps.

When we got drafted, we went to Boston for a physical and aptitude tests. I went home to wait for my number to come up. We got processed at Fort Devens. I ended up going to Camp Chaffee at Fort Smith, Arkansas. It was an artillery base. That was sixteen weeks of basic—eight weeks of general infantry training and then they put us on the 105s [105 millimeter artillery gun] for eight weeks of basic artillery. I ended up being a squad leader simply because they took the tallest guy who could march reasonably well and put him at the head of the column.

Basic wasn't too bad. We had the physical work—an obstacle course and hikes—during the first eight weeks. We used the carbine. We didn't have the M1. [Both the carbine and the M1 are 30-caliber weapons. The carbine is lighter, its cartridges shorter

Although it seemed to **ARTHUR P. "ART" TAROLLI, in camp in Korea, that the action was probably over, he would soon experience intense trench warfare.**
and its bullets lighter than the M1. Because the shells are lighter, a man could carry more. The M1 had a longer range with its longer cartridge and heavier bullet. Officers frequently carried carbines and enlisted infantry men carried the M1.]

During the second eight weeks, we learned the loading, firing, and range finding, and the whole bit on the 105. At the end of the sixteen weeks, if all the tests you had taken indicated you had something that they were looking for, you were given the option of going to leadership school for another eight weeks. It was NCO [Non-Commissioned Officers] school. I can't remember if I was asked or told I was going to leadership school, but, anyway, I went.

In November of 1951, the UN and Communist negotiators agreed to a truce line roughly along the thirty-eighth parallel. The announcement said they planned to have a full armistice within thirty days. The announcement did not bear fruit. In January of 1952 a proposed armistice offer was rejected because the North Koreans refused a ban on building new air fields in the North. The war would go on for another year and a half.

Going to NCO school was the preliminary step for going to OCS (Officer Candidate School). You could turn it down if you weren't interested. You didn't have to go. But you knew what it meant when they said, "What assignment would you like? Which officer candidate school would you prefer to go to?" I put down three choices. Fort Monmouth, in New Jersey, was a popular choice with the East Coast guys. It was nearby, so I put down signal corps [the specialty of Fort Monmouth]. I didn't know anything about signal corps.

The second choice was Fort Sill, Oklahoma. One of the choices had to be one of the combat arms: armor, infantry, like that. Everybody shied away from the infantry. There was a war going on. Of course, most of us ended up at Fort Benning, Georgia, the infantry school. That's where I went to OCS: Fort Benning, Georgia. That was twenty-two weeks during the summer of 1952. The training at Benning, in the middle of the summertime, was tougher than basic. That summer was exceptionally hot. One of the basic goals of officer candidate school is to teach the leaders to build teamwork and responsibility to the group.

> **I ended up being a squad leader simply because they took the tallest guy who could march reasonably well and put him at the head of the column. Basic wasn't too bad. We had the physical work—an obstacle course and hikes—during the first eight weeks.**

Win or lose, sports teach that everyone must do his part if the team is to succeed. They tried to instill pride in the unit. We had a drill team. We had an excellent softball team. That was amazing when you figure we had just come together. We got one guy from here and one from there, and the coach was a fellow from Gilbertville, [Massachusetts], Joseph Valardi. Ironically, his cubical was just across from mine, and I had known him before we were drafted. The week before we graduated, our team won the Fort Benning championship. Had we not graduated, we would have gone on to the Third Army championship tournament. The second place team, the ones we beat, Medical Company, represented Benning.

Continuing to build pride in the team and responsibility to each other, Art's unit created their own project.

We had a day room. One of the guys suggested we use the local bamboo to panel the lower half of the day room. We cut it down and varnished it. When we got through, it was the best looking day room at Fort Benning. We did that in addition to the training and all the baloney.

At Benning, they gave us an M1. We were supposed to know how to take it apart, put it together, and know the manual of arms with it. But we'd had only the carbine at Chaffee. The M1 was an experience and a half. We had evaluations every five or six weeks. We probably lost nearly half of the number we started with before we graduated. Everybody had to write an evaluation on each other in the squad. The officers used those and also rated each of us. After the ratings, we went before a board. If you didn't cut it, you were gone.

While we were going through OCS, we had the rank of sergeant. If someone got boarded out, he went back to the rank he had before he got there. Some of the guys intentionally got themselves boarded out. Remember, there was a war going on. Not too many were gung-ho and wanted to go. They kept pounding into our heads how short the life span of a platoon leader was and how responsible you'd have to be.

Some of the guys had the intention to stay in OCS right up until the end and then get themselves boarded out. They hoped to get sent to Europe. Not everyone was going to the Far East. Some of them pulled it off. They made it right up to the last two or three weeks and said

On Duty...
Geography
Art Tarolli

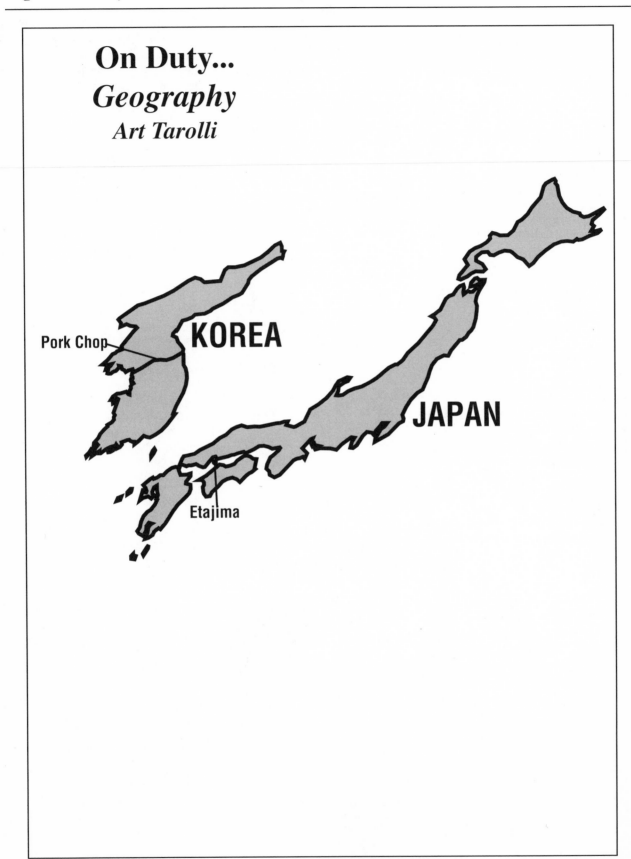

they didn't want to be an officer. Well, if you didn't want to be an officer, they didn't want you. Some of the guys were lucky enough to get sent to Germany. OCS was tough, and some of the guys just didn't make it.

The last two weeks, we were called senior candidates, and we got to wear a blue helmet liner. That indicated you were only a step away from becoming a second lieutenant. As senior candidates, we'd go out to the rest of the companies, and we were officers as far as they were concerned. And after taking it for twenty weeks—I mean TAKING it—some couldn't wait to give it out. I felt sorry for some of those kids who were catching it. The blue hats took out twenty weeks of frustration in those last two weeks. It was quite an experience. Before that, if we saw those guys with the blue hats coming, brother look out, and stay clear. If we met one, we had to salute him. They were officers as far as the underclassmen were concerned. I think we graduated 120 out of more than two hundred who started together.

I graduated from OCS 12 September 1952, one year to the day since I went into the service. The graduation ceremony included a parade. They called each man up and presented us with bars—it was impressive. I went home on leave. Then I was assigned to a duty station, Fort Leonard Wood, Missouri, awaiting my overseas assignment. I got there in the fall— October of 1952. I was a training officer. I just put in my time teaching classes in weaponry

and tactics. I lived in the BOQ [bachelor officer quarters]. Then in March, I got my orders to go overseas. Again, I got some leave and went home.

I flew to Japan on Northwest Airlines. We landed on a little island at the very end of the Aleutian Islands—Shemya. I didn't know Shemya from shoe-me-ya. We landed. It was dark when we got out. It was desolate—nothing. It's just a teeny-weeny little speck. We stayed there for a few hours and then resumed our flight. I think it was just a refueling stop. Then we went on to Japan.

We landed in Tokyo, probably Tachikawa Air Base, and from there went on to Camp Drake. That was the Army processing center. At Camp Drake, they issued uniforms, more fatigues, and equipment. When we left the States, we had dress uniforms and a couple of pairs of fatigues. At Drake, they gave us more fatigues and equipment we'd need in the field. Also after leaving Drake, we went through the CBR [chemical, biological, and radiological] school for a couple of weeks. That was at Etajima near Hiroshima. As a matter of fact, we visited Hiroshima. Ground Zero, the center of the impact of the atomic bomb, is an exhibition hall. What's left of the hall is preserved as a memorial. The CBR school was pretty "cinchy." There wasn't much to it. It was like they were just killing time until we got assignments to Korea. It was pretty basic stuff.

Then we got assignments to where we were actually going in Korea. I got assigned to the Seventh Division. From divi-

sion, we went to regiment for indoctrination, and then on down to the rifle company. We had three rifle platoons and a weapons platoon. They had beefed up the squads—had extra people in them. Ideally, there are about two hundred in a company, fifty to a platoon. SOP [standard operating procedure], according to the manual, has from ten to twelve men to a squad and four squads to a platoon. Then there are the other personnel—radio men and specialists—so there are two hundred in a company.

I got assigned to the second platoon. I was platoon leader of the second platoon, Easy Company, Thirty-second Infantry Regiment. When I was taken to meet the company commander, it was my first experience with the hills of Korea. The old man was living up top at the CP [command post]. They said, "Okay. Let's go." There were stairs cut out in the hill. I had my gear. The stairs, luckily, went from one side to the other. Straight up would have been nearly impossible. Anyway, we got up there.

We went into the bunker. The commander's name was Jack Thun, a Korean-American. He was a soldier all the way. I found out later that it was his third tour of duty in Korea. He made sergeant during his first tour. He went again and earned a battlefield commission. He made captain on his third tour. Rank comes fast in war time. I'm a case in point— making first lieutenant much faster than I ordinarily would have.

A lot of career men had volunteered. Some of them were

not happy when the war ended, simply because the rank was coming fast and furious. A guy goes over there as a second lieutenant and in no time at all, he's a captain. There was no waiting period. Jack Thun had risen quickly. He was a very good soldier and a very strict disciplinarian. He didn't take any crap from anybody. He ran his company the way it should be run. It was kind of intimidating for a while.

The second platoon was a rifle platoon. Captain Thun wasn't happy with the guy who had the platoon before and transferred him to the motor pool. So he got out of the front line. The company was on the MLR [main line of resistance]. By then the war had stabilized. It wasn't very fluid. It was more a throwback to World War I. That was the spring of 1953. The war ended 27 July 1953.

It was a stable, almost trench war. We were on line, and you could look across the valley, and they were over there. It was all patrol activity unless somebody made a move, and we weren't taking any initiatives at that time. They had been talking at Panmunjom since 1951. We didn't want to be the aggressor. Any offensive moves were made by the Chinese. And most of them [the enemy] were Chinese by then [not Korean]. There may have been a few North Koreans sprinkled around here and there, but they [the enemy forces] were all Chinese divisions and regiments.

We just held our ground. When I got to my platoon, they were all dug in. There were permanent trenches—nothing slipshod. The trenches were constructed using twelve by twelves. They were well constructed bunkers. They were permanent fortifications. I'd have to send out an ambush patrol or a reconnaissance patrol in the rice paddies between the two lines—ours and theirs. That's the kind of warfare it was.

Once in a while we'd get harassing fire, artillery fire—a few artillery rounds just to keep us honest. And we'd do the same to them. There was no big action in front of us. There was action on other points of the line. We'd hear that the Marines got hit over there or the Chinese went after an outpost somewhere. We lost a few men from artillery or lost some on patrols—they got ambushed—but nothing huge.

The company that I was in, E Company, had been hit prior to my getting there. They were involved in some pretty good fire fights. Ambush patrols were kind of hairy. We'd go out at night, perhaps two thousand yards. We'd set up along a known or theoretical trail. The idea being that, if the Chinese sent out a patrol that went along that trail, we'd ambush them. I never had to do that.

Once in a while our men did make contact. There was a fire fight, and we lost some people. We had barbed wire and mines out in front of our trenches. We threw all the cans from the rations out in front of us. If someone walked there, you'd hear, *klink, klink*. Once in a while an animal—a rabbit—would make a noise. We had lines of fire established in case we got hit. We test fired the weapons every other day. It got boring after a while.

We got chow with another company on our right flank. We had to eat in back of a hill. Our guys had mobile kitchens, and the food was hot. A lot of the food was brought in by truck. We didn't get hot meals all the time. We got to learn to like the regular rations. There were signs on the side of the road going to the chow area, "Joe Chink can see you." At that point of the road, there was no cover and the Chinese could look right across. They knew when we went to chow. They knew when to fire in a few artillery shells.

They had 105s and 155s— big stuff. Our 105s and 155s were back toward the reserve area behind the hills. They weren't used for direct fire. I guess they did use them for direct fire before I got there when the situation was more mobile. Our artillery would fire over our heads. And our guys dug in the tanks on the ridges in such a way so we could run the tanks up and fire the "quad-fifties" just for harassing fire. The tanks would get off a few rounds, and then they would back off.

The artillery units had targets all picked out, and they'd fire harassing fire all night long. The Chinese did the same thing to us. Our platoon was on the MLR for fifty-eight days, almost two months. Other than patrol activity, we took no aggressive action.

After two months on line, it was our turn to go back in reserve. Another company came up to take our place. Nobody had been bloodied up too badly.

I was there in the summer. When it rained, it really rained. Bunkers would cave in. Every once in a while, we were warned to check for water damage so nothing would collapse. Fortunately, I wasn't there in the winter. Winters up north were bad. Our quarters on the line were the trenches. The fighting trench was open, and the covered trench was protected with substantial amounts of earth. Every so many feet of trench had a bunker. That's where we slept. The covered trenches and bunkers had apertures where we could fire. My command-post bunker had three bunks for my first sergeant, my radio man, and me. The other bunkers each had two men.

When we went in reserve, we had tents. Reserve was comfortably behind where the Chinese artillery was dropping. The whole company went back and breathed a sigh of relief.

Our Air Force was doing some work then, but their air force hardly existed. It had evolved into a strange war. There were strange, almost gentlemanly-like rules. We didn't fly over the Yalu River. They didn't fly behind our lines. [General Douglas] MacArthur got in his jam because of such strange rules. So as soon as we got behind the MLR, no problem. They could drop artillery shells on the MLR. It would have been nothing to raise the guns a couple of clicks and drop the shells over the hills. [Artillery pieces had a control knob that rotated to raise or lower the barrel. As the knob was turned, each notch (click) represented a known distance that the shell would

fly.] A thousand yards north, there was a war going on. In the rear we could shower when we felt like it and get clean clothes. We could go down to a shower point where guys walked around with no helmets on. Every company in reserve had an assignment. We were in reserve, but if something happened, we had a job. We figured that was no problem. We thought the war would be over in a few weeks.

I remember when Thun said we had to go and look at [a hill called] Pork Chop.

Dressed as if for battle, Art wore fifty pounds of gear. He would tote it while leading his platoon up steep Korean hills and into combat.

I said, "Why?"

He said it was our assignment in case something happened. He said if they needed us, "We go."

I thought, "Yeah. Yeah." They were talking peace, and I figured nothing was going to happen. If something did start,

our company would be the first one to go. It didn't seem to bother us very much. Nobody expected anything.

Pork Chop had been lost and retaken in April before I got there. That's what the book was written about and what they made the movie from. It was just a small hill. It was exposed and outflanked. We had lost [hills called] Old Baldy on one side and T-Bone on the other side. Pork Chop was standing out all by itself. It was a hill about the size of Tully Mountain [in Tully, Massachusetts]. It should have never been defended the way it was. Politically, it was a chip. They were in the midst of the peace talks, and every little chip or pawn gave them leverage at the [peace talk] tables. The Chinese had made up their minds that they wanted that chip.

We went out and looked it over. They gave us glasses [binoculars] and a map of the hill. We decided the route we would take. Most of it went in one ear and out the other. The war was almost over. It was a formality that had to be taken care of, and I understood that. We got the briefing out of the way and got back to the company rear. We were playing cards, just relaxing.

Down the road, there were two artillery batteries—a 105 and a 155 [105-millimeter and 155-millimeter artillery guns]. They would fire once in a while, mostly at night—just harassing fire. Then one night, after we had gone to bed, the two batteries were firing. It was more than harassing fire.

The firing was constant. No stopping. I thought, "Oh, Oh.

Something's happening." The Chinese had hit Pork Chop. That's what all the artillery was about. We were blasting the hell out of the Chinese attack. The Chinese had committed everything they had in the vicinity to take the hill. We got the call in the middle of the night. We had to go. It was raining, pouring. And we had to go—go up that hill. I'm telling you, thinking about it still gives me goose bumps now.

We went. We got up there. By the time we got briefed and squared away at regiment, it was just breaking daylight. All hell was breaking loose. Artillery from both sides were pounding that little anthill. It was nothing but a pile of dirt. All the fortifications and trenches had been reconstructed after the April encounter. Our guys had built new trenches, command post, and fortifications—really built it up and reinforced it. The Americans figured they weren't going to lose it again.

Both sides were pounding the hell out of it, and there was only one access road. That was it. It went from behind in the sheltered area, out into the open, and up to where they'd unload us at Pork Chop. We went. Between eight and ten guys got into each APC [armored personnel carrier]. Going up over that road, we could hear the bullets banging off that carrier.

Talk about scared! And scared about what we'd find when they let us out. We knew there was a stretch of covered trench and a stretch of open. Off those were the fighting trenches. The main trench was

designed to withstand anything they could throw. But, if several shells hit the same place over and over again, there was not much to keep them from breaking through. When they opened those APC doors, there in front of us was the opening [into the covered trenches]. We only had to go from here to there [fifteen feet]. It was just like going into a mole hole. They opened the doors, and we jumped out. There was smoke all over the place and screaming and yelling. It had been raining, and the mud was thick all over.

When they opened the doors, lying right there was an American soldier—dead! It was, "Let's go." We had to step right over him.

Slowly, but surely, they eventually got the whole company up there that way. But talk about confusion, panic, or whatever you want to call it. Here's this other company that was hit, all banged up, all shot up trying to get evacuated. They were coming down the trench while we were trying to go up, and there wasn't that much room. What a mess. Radios were squawking. The Chinese where blowing the hell out of our side with their artillery, and we were blowing the hell out of their side with our artillery.

That was a Tuesday morning. They hit on Monday night, the sixth of July. The orders came down, "Move ahead." Our job was to secure that part of the hill the Chinese hadn't taken. It was like that until Friday. That's the kind of job it was for four days—trying to get the wounded guys off and the

new guys on. Other companies had to sweep the hill, trying to regain area.

Fortunately, we were in the trenches. The guys who had to sweep the hill got chewed up company after company. You may have seen the movie and read the book, but you never heard about those guys getting chewed up.

During that battle, Art's actions earned the Silver Star. The citation reads in part, *Second Lieutenant ARTHUR P. TAROLLI ...leading his men in a counterattack against strategic enemy-held positions... displayed gallantry [that] reflects great credit on himself and is in keeping with the highest traditions of the military service.*

Upon landing his platoon, the citation continues, *Lt....Tarolli organized and personally supervised each fighting position in the area he was assigned. Lt. Tarolli joined the assault group and advanced through the dark, enemy infested, covered trench. As he passed a junction controlled by the enemy and turned a sharp corner, the group was taken under intense enemy fire, delivered through gaps in the overhead cover and from blown out bunkers. Three men were wounded and blocked the area. Lt. Tarolli remained, evacuated his wounded and immediately organized another group... .*

The citation explains that Art and his group persevered in the assault and then built a barricade in the trench to use supporting fire. Art supervised construction of the barricade and also accomplished evacuation of his group's wounded.

Art sees himself as a man who did his job and reluctantly related the details that earned the citation.

When the order came to move up, parts of the trench were controlled by the Chinese. One particular turn became obnoxious. We couldn't get around it. There was a Chinese soldier with a burp gun that we couldn't detect. A burp gun is a light weight, small caliber, fully automatic weapon ideal for short range, in close fighting. Firing a burst of shots sounded like a "burp."

Everything was caved in, wrecked, beams falling down, sandbags spilling, and he was concealed. Every time we tried to get around the corner, he'd open up with the burp gun. We couldn't get around. A couple of our guys had been wounded there. We decided to try to use a rifle grenade. We knew approximately where he was.

I got one of the guys in the squad with a grenade launcher. In those days, you put the launcher right on your rifle, and the grenade had a protective cap. When the M1 fired, it launched the grenade. Unless the cap was removed from the grenade, it wouldn't go off. In the heat of battle, the kid poked around the corner and fired the grenade with the cap still on. It landed right around the corner, but didn't go off.

The flamethrower was the next option. I called him up. He stuck the flamethrower around and threw off a few bursts. He never realized the grenade hadn't gone off and was still lying there around the corner. After a few bursts with the flamethrower, the grenade got hot enough and went off. We were all around the corner and protected. By accident or whatever, when the flames settled down and we poked our heads around, there was no problem. We either scared the guy away or blew him away: it didn't matter. That was the most difficult situation we had that day. We threw up a sandbag barricade on that corner, and I put a couple of guys behind it. Then we moved our way up the trench.

As we did, we ran into people who had been left from the initial attack. We heard some people moaning and yelling, "Help!" There were three who had been hit the day before, but not evacuated. We got them down. We were relatively safe in the trenches. The guys who were sweeping the hill took the heaviest casualties. The only way they could get cover was to get into our trenches. We'd pull them into the trench or send somebody out to get them when they got hit. Then we could evacuate them through our trench line. The trench was not wide, and it was full of our people, and, for two or three days, litters were end to end the whole length of the trench, more than a hundred yards all the way down to the evacuation command post.

They used the same APCs that brought the troops up to take the wounded back. There was only that one access to the hill. The Chinese controlled the flanks, Baldy, and T-Bone. Those on Baldy looked right down on that road and, obviously, it wasn't too hard to see what was happening. They could reach the access road with everything they had.

The Army was forced to alert the Twenty-fifth Division, which was in reserve, to back up our Seventh Division. The Seventeenth Infantry Regiment and my Thirty-second had been badly chewed up. Very little was written about that July encounter. Defeats are not usually glorified. The Chinese took substantial losses.

They were on the outside while we were in the trenches. The guy on the outside, trying to take, is more exposed. We had a tactic called "flash fires." Before Pork Chop was hit, we planned how we would flash the hill if it was ever necessary. All the coordinates were zeroed in. Everything that was in range of Pork Chop: the 105s, 155s, tanks, .50-caliber machine guns along the ridge anything that could reach the hill had their coordinates all prearranged. If the command came, "Flash Pork Chop," everybody who could reach it fired for a predetermined amount of time—say fifteen minutes. When Chinese got on the hill, the guys in the trenches were given a warning that the "flash" was coming. Our guys went turtle—got under as much cover as we could find. They let everything go—our own fire right on top of us.

Talk about scary! Everything was coming in, everything shaking. I had to wonder how many hits our cover could take. They had to "flash" Pork Chop twice while we were there. What a waste!

Dick Shea was probably the greatest track star West Point ever had—a miler. He was a platoon leader on the hill. He was going around trying to gather up people, because an order had come down for his unit to attack. He was a West Pointer, gung-ho. He gathered up a few and took off. I found out later he got the Congressional Medal of Honor posthumously. I read later that his baby was born two days after he got killed on that hill. Shea Stadium at West Point is named after him.

They pulled us off the hill Friday night. We had been there ninety hours. The next day, the order came down, "Abandon Pork Chop." We couldn't retain it, and they couldn't take it. It was one of those in-between jobs. But the Chinese were successful. They had done what they wanted to do, which was to get us off. Before that battle, we had the hill. That was just another chip.

That was the tenth of July. On the eleventh, we were back in the company area. We rested a day, got cleaned up, and took positions in back of Pork Chop on Hill 200 [so named because it is two-hundred meters high]. Sunday the twelfth was a crystal clear, bluebird day. The Air Force and Navy fighter bombers were called out. They dive bombed what was left of Pork Chop with one-thousand-pounders. That went on all that morning. They just pounded it to smithereens. When the

bombing ended, it was just a pile of dirt. A costly pile of dirt.

We took up positions on Hill 200 and went out on patrols, but the Chinese were apparently satisfied with what they had done. There was no more offensive action in that area. There was still action on other parts of the MLR, but they didn't bother us anymore. We kind of waited it out until the war ended. We received the Stars & Stripes [GI newspaper] and got the word about what was happening at Panmunjom. They were getting closer and closer to signing. The closer it got to signing, the more we were apprehensive about being the last ones to get killed. That's how we went through those final two weeks.

Newspaper headlines on 28 July 1953 read, *Shooting Stops in Korea and Armistice Signed*.

It was a strange ending for a strange war. We were told they had signed the papers at ten o'clock on the morning of the twenty-seventh. So, the truce was signed. The provision was that the shooting would not stop until ten o'clock that night.

So the war was over, but the shooting would go on for another twelve hours. That was a tough twelve hours. The word was, "Stay under cover. Don't even go out to eat." The Chinese were playing games. They'd fire flares to give the impression they were cooking up something. They had used that [firing flares] before attacks sometimes. They were playing mind games during that twelve hours. They had always been the ones doing the offen-

sive stuff. They made us sweat it out right to the end.

When it ended, it was, "Okay. Rip everything down. Wreck it." We went to Hill 200 to rip out the bunkers and fill in the trenches. Again, it was all done by hand. We had no machines. The Chinese were all over Pork Chop. They were waving flags, playing music through speakers. They would walk right down to the bottom of the ravine, which was half way.

We had strict orders, "Don't go anywhere near them." So we were there watching them as they yelled, "Come on down" and played American songs. Two days before, they were trying to kill us. They knew how to play the mind games. After we de-constructed Hill 200, we went back into reserve. I saw a picture in *Life* magazine. The photographer took the picture from Hill 200 while we were taking down the fortifications. He had a picture of the Chinese down in the valley between us, waving the flags. My radio man happened to be standing beside me at the time, and he's in the foreground of that *Life* magazine picture. Nice picture of the back of his helmet, and I was right next to him, but he didn't get me in the photograph.

That picture and a whole spread appeared in *Life* magazine. When I look at that picture, I can't believe how many people were sacrificed for that hill. It just wasn't worth it. It looks like a handful of sand, piled up and rounded off. What could be so important, to chew up that many lives? It was just a bargaining chip. The Chinese just wanted to be able to say they straightened the line out. It gave them a little more leverage at the bargaining table. It was a hell of a reason for such a sacrifice. When they ended the war, each side had to pull back a mile and a quarter, so the DMZ [Demilitarized Zone] is two and a half miles wide, if I remember correctly. All the places: Pork Chop, Baldy, Hill 200 are within the DMZ.

As if to confirm Arthur's contention that rank comes faster in war time, he was promoted to first lieutenant.

We spent the rest of the summer building fortifications on another MLR below the DMZ in case something broke out later. They flew in big twelve-by-twelve beams by helicopter. We were building permanent bunker fortifications. Then we went further into reserve, down around Seoul.

We took part in operation "Big Switch," where we exchanged our prisoners for their prisoners. Each of their prisoners had to be interviewed to see if he wanted to stay with the Communists or return, and each of our prisoners had to be interviewed to see if he wanted to go back. We loaded them [the North Korean and Chinese prisoners] onto trains and took them back to the area where they were going to be interviewed. Some of them, North Koreans mostly, decided not to go back. There were twenty-four from our side who decided not to come back. For whatever reason, they wanted to stay with the Chinese. Most of them, later, came back.

Twenty-seven thousand North Korean prisoners refused to return to their homes.

Twenty-three Americans and one British soldier refused repatriation after the armistice.

There might have been a couple that were truly philosophically convinced the Chinese way was better, but, ultimately, most of them ended up coming back or died up there.

There were an awful lot of MIAs—men who didn't get home and weren't proved to have been killed. My wife and I went to the Punch Bowl Memorial Cemetery in Hawaii. I was amazed. Guys that I had heard about from my OCS company were killed in action. Their names were there. They died on Pork Chop. I had assumed they were killed and their bodies recovered. I found they were listed as MIA, missing in action, and presumed dead. They were never found. Their names were on that memorial. A lot of them, obviously, got buried on the hill, right there. Thousands throughout Korea were never officially found. They were buried there.

They had always drummed it into our heads, "Don't ever leave a body behind." That's good, but there are times when that is impossible to do. Common sense needs to take over. It's great to go get them and bring them back, but at what cost? On Pork Chop, it was simply impossible to retrieve some of those people. There were people who had been hit before they flashed Pork Chop. After they flashed the hill, there was nothing there.

Big Switch took place in September. Soon after we got through escorting prisoners, we did routine training. The war was over. And when a war is

over, they don't need you any more. My hitch was due to end in March. When I graduated from OCS, I had to sign for an eighteen-month commitment, so I was due to get out in March.

Then they came down and said people who wanted to get out early could get out. I wasn't a career soldier, so I said, "Absolutely. The sooner, the better."

In December, before Christmas, I got released. I came back on a ship, a military job, but I can't remember its name. It was packed with guys coming back, and it wasn't fancy. It took us a couple of weeks. We got off and went to Camp Stoneman, California. After a day or two, we got on a train and came across the country to the Worcester station. It was still operating then. My mother was there to pick me up. Shortly after that, I was out-processed at Fort Devens. The date of discharge was 11 December 1953.

Because of military service, I had the GI Bill [financial education assistance for veterans of the armed services]. I had done some teaching at Fort Leonard Wood, and I enjoyed it. Some of my friends were going to teachers' college at Fitchburg [State College, in Fitchburg, Massachusetts]. I took a ride down with them and talked to the dean. I didn't have to take an entrance exam, and I started the end of January, 1954. That's when I met my wife. Going to school summers, I graduated in 1957. The rest is history.

And Arthur taught history at Athol High School for the next thirty-two years.

Donald Corser Of Royalston

United States Navy, 1926-1930; 1942-1943
United States Coast Guard, 1930-1933

Always At Home On The Bounding Main

Fresh in sailor's middy, DONALD CORSER saw the world from his place on deck.

After graduation from Athol High School in 1926, Donald Corser set out to seek his fortune. The sea soon called.

A friend was in New England Mutual Life Insurance in Boston. He offered, "How would you like to go into life insurance?"

Cows and hoeing peas were getting old so, I said, "Yes." I didn't last at all. In those days, they paid kids starting in the insurance business, boys in the stock exchange, and kids in the bank a universal fifty dollars a month. I paid seven dollars a week board. It was cutting it pretty fine. I was a little crowded. It wasn't for me—the streetcars, subways.

I boarded out in Dorchester. It was quite a trip. I worked in the mail department. I'd carry the locked bag, the good stuff they didn't throw in the truck, to the post office. And I'd see all the posters of guys looking out to sea with the wind in their hair. I said, "What to hell?" So I shipped in. Zippo—down to Newport to boot camp.

It was called "boot camp" because that was the uniform of the day for new recruits—rubber boots up to the knees. After you got the shots, you were quarantined for twenty-one days. You shouldn't go out and lay it on other people, so you were quarantined to a certain area. After twenty-one days, we were allowed in the general population, but not the ship's company, of course. They were the elite. Boot camp was a minimum of eight weeks. The old timers didn't have to wear the boots any more. They had two or three months in the Navy. They were salty.

The company commander was a chief petty officer, a guy named Flagg. We drove him crazy. We learned basic seamanship. Later, I used to teach the Boy Scouts—splices and knots, all that. And, wintertime, now: pulling an open boat, eight-man cutters with twelve-foot oars. And military courtesy—like when you pass an officer on deck, you must be down wind. That goes way back to the sailing days. The lower ranking man couldn't pass his stink to an officer, so he had to be down wind. We learned rules like going forward on the starboard and aft on the port. That's why, when they have an accelerated program, like in time of war, there is a lot of confusion, because they skip those parts of the training. You wonder how they ever won the war. All that program has a grounding. When you tell some kid to grab a broom and crumb up the area, the kid doesn't say "I don't work for you."

The choice of schools available to today's Navy personnel didn't exist then.

We had machinist mate school, torpedo school, pharmacist's mate school, diving school, and a few others. There was an opening in the pharmacist's mate school, so I said, "I'll do it." I figured I could swab a little iodine. That rate could become quite a thing.

But I didn't get to become quite a thing. I got measles. One evening right after chow, I saw all these spots. I didn't feel sick, but I went to sick bay. I didn't get out of sick bay. I was quarantined. And I really wasn't a good pharmacist's mate student. It wasn't like high school. If you were serious and could really do it, it was okay, but I really wasn't a good student. When that Number 21 jumped, I was quarantined.

Any quarantine for shots

or measles was for twenty-one days.

Not being in the top half of the class by any means, and getting that far behind, there was no way. "Lord, send me to sea."

We had guys who had been to sea, and they suggested, "You don't want any of that sea stuff." But I went to yard tugs at Norfolk. They had good food, and I was a seaman second class.

Yard tugs were tug boats too small to warrant their own name. They were identified by a number. After working on several and letting his preference for sea be known, Don got his wish.

A guy came up looking for me. "Go up to the yeoman's office. They've got word for you up there." So up I went.

"Get your gear together, Corser. You're leaving." I was assigned to the *Kittery*, one of the two last coal-burning ships in the Navy. She was a transport that had been taken over from Germany. And off to Haiti. That was my first foreign port. I was pretty salty by then.

They put me on shore patrol with a brassard, squeegee handle. Just picture me telling some big old bos'n mate on his fourth cruise, "Hey, Mac. Square your hat." Just see me doing that. What we had were Marines on Haiti, Nicaragua, and all over the area. We still should have. They had it bottled up good. I always think of those Marines, because they had to eat on the top side. Their food

was served, and they ate off the hatch covers. The wind blew their soup all over their clothes. Good stuff.

At Guantanamo Bay, Cuba, he got a change of assignment. He caught the sta-

> **Boot camp was a minimum of eight weeks. We learned basic seamanship: splices and knots, pulling an open boat. And military courtesy. We learned rules like going forward on the starboard and aft on the port. That's why, when they have an accelerated program, like in time of war, there is a lot of confusion, because they skip those parts of the training.**

tion ship, a seagoing tug.

I did a year on her. We had two channels to take care of. Cuba was a protectorate at the time. We handled the buoys. It was fun. The lights were carbide; when water was added, it made a gas that burned and made the light. We took care of the Media Luna Channel. One time, we towed a vessel that was carrying our skipper's furniture. Our ship was the *Montcalm*, and our skipper was a chief warrant officer. [There were only two classes of warrant then: warrant and chief warrant]. Our skipper was Jorgenson. Our ship was Jorgey's Yacht. The paint was off all the brass, and there was a lot of bright work. We towed a vessel that had Jorgey's furniture on her, and we ran into

a hurricane. At times, she was off to our port, and at times, she was off to the starboard side, and all the time, Jorgey was tearing his hair out, but we got her in okay.

When a crewman from the *Memphis* boarded Jorgey's Yacht looking for manpower, Don's résumé expanded.

Their guy wanted a swap. The *Memphis* was six-hundred-plus feet long, fifty-seven-foot beam, had twelve six-inch .53-caliber guns [108-pound shells], four three-inch .50-calibre guns, two twenty-four-inch triple torpedo tubes, four boats, and two Corsair *Scout* bi-wing planes. [The *Scout* planes were catapulted off. When they returned, they landed on the water and were lifted back onto the deck.] The *Memphis* had a crew of three hundred-odd. Anyway, I swapped on to her.

From Guantanamo, we went through the Panama Canal. You go into a lock, and on either side of the canal, there were electric mules with lines going from the ship to the mules. There were three sets of lifts on each end with Gatun Lake in the middle. On the merchant ships, the crew would man the winch and the pilot would signal to wind, but the electric mules prevent the ship from wrecking the lock. For a long part of it, there are no locks. It's a river, a cut, the Culebra Cut. We were part of the crew, later, that took the *Saratoga* aircraft carrier through. She had only a foot clearance on either side. The Atlantic side is actually farther west than the Pacific side, the way the thing lays. One time, we were going through, and I was running a winch, a fellow asked if I had been through the canal before.

On Duty...
Geography
Don Corser

When I said it was my sixteenth time, he said, "Well, then. You wouldn't be interested in any immoral literature."

Going through the Panama Canal more than a dozen times, Don learned the ropes and got "salty." His ship, the USS *Memphis*, makes the passage, above.

After getting through the canal, the next stop was Hawaii and then on to China.

The first place we made on the China coast was Chefoo. We were on the North China patrol, anywhere from the Manchurian border on down to Hong Kong. On our own, we went to Macao or Canton. At that time, China was in a state of flux. They weren't Communist. Mao and Chiang Kai Shek were jockeying for power. A fellow named Herbert Hoover owned a lot of shares in a mining corporation up against the Manchurian border. I wonder why we were there.

We'd patrol in undressed blues [standard Navy uniform with no stripes or insignia—working clothes]. We men who were further south dyed whites in coffee.

White uniforms stood out brightly. Dyeing the whites in coffee was their version of camouflage.

Parts of China were owned by Standard Oil. Everybody was there except the Chinese. There was the Fifth Regiment of Marines and the Fifteenth Infantry, who had been there since the Boxer Rebellion. Then there where some people there, the French Foreign Legion from Lao Boa. Then Vietnam, Laos, and Cambodia were all French Indo China. I guess we got it done. I don't recall any shots fired in anger.

We got out of there in the winter. The area would freeze up, and the ship would have been stuck there. There was an outfit in Shanghai, China, made up of mostly civilians, multinationals. They were a paramilitary group like the old Hudson Bay Army.

In the China Sea, we saw a squadron of Japanese destroyers that were very much in evidence wherever we went. We made two trips to Japan. One was Emperor Hirohito's coronation and his birthday. We ran around the Imperial Palace yelling "Banzai, Banzai," and we toured the sights including the largest Buddha in the world, in Kamakura, Japan.

The China tour lasted for about two years.

After you were out for as much as two years, you flew a homeward-bound pennant. Everybody on the ship got a piece of the pennant when you finally made home port. The pennant

Before muster with his shipmates in China, above, Don was assigned to patrolling near Standard Oil installations, background. Don and his mates referred to Standard Oil factory as a "seventeen-stack cruiser."

had white stars on a blue field, one star for each officer and, theoretically, a foot of red and white stripe for each enlisted man. You'd fly it when you left the station until you reached home port. I guess you could call our home port Norfolk, but they were not too hot on us. Our skipper was from Baltimore. He got us home ported there, and that was great. They didn't see the Navy men that often, so the treatment was "good stuff."

By 1931, the "enlistment" was up. Don got paid off in Boston and was again a civilian. Land couldn't keep its hold.

Another friend influenced me in to shipping into the Coast Guard. We went up to the Customs House in Boston to get a physical for an AB ticket [designating able bodied seaman] and a lifeboat ticket from the Coast Guard to allow me to work as a merchant seaman. There was a guy from Athol, Merton Lilly, who worked in the doctor's office. When I said I wanted to work on merchant ships, he said, "How about the Coast Guard?."

I said, "How about the Coast Guard!"

He said it was a pretty good outfit. So I went up to the fifteenth floor in the Customs House to talk with them. Bye and bye, I was over at the chief yeoman's desk. A little while later, I met a fellow I knew, and he said, "What have you done?"

I said, "Why?"

He said, "You're going to the *Tampa*." I thought that was okay—sunshine and all.

He said, "No, no. THE *Tampa!*" She was a Coast Guard cutter working in the North Atlantic. The Coast Guard was then under the treasury department. Our duties were two-fold: protection of life and property at sea and enforcement of the Internal Revenue Act, which meant, grab people bringing in bad stuff. There wasn't any marijuana then; I guess people did smoke it, but no one paid attention to it. Booze was just dying—looking bad.

So the North Atlantic patrol blew up a whale that was floating around—a menace to navigation. And monitored ice. We weren't on ice patrol; the ships doing ice patrol did twenty and ten [twenty days at sea and ten in port] out of Halifax. If we came on a berg, we would monitor it, but that wasn't our mission. I didn't fare well in that vessel at all. She was three hundred feet long, maybe four thousand tons. I hadn't been out of the Navy that long, so I could get my rate back. I applied for any ship or station. Just to get the hell out of the North Atlantic Coast Guard.

It didn't work, but the exec threatened that the next time anyone came up before him, that person would be gone. I infringed something, I don't remember what: pissed into the wind or something. I got transferred to a patrol craft chasing people in a dying industry running of rum. I did about a year in that and then out. A civilian!!

As a civilian again, Don still sought his labors at sea. With his AB ticket, he signed on as a merchant seaman.

I worked for Standard Oil, Continental, Ward Line—the outfit that the Morro Castle belonged to. It was burned up off Asbury Park, New Jersey. Our runs for Standard Oil would go everywhere: South America, Aruba, and Dutch West Indies. On the west coast, we'd sea load [if the tanker was too large to get into the harbor, the oil was piped or brought out by smaller ships] from El Segundo and that area. In Venezuela, we loaded mostly in a jungle river. There, we couldn't take a full load. We'd take part of the load, and a mosquito fleet of smaller tankers would top us off. And I worked for lumber companies—the last one was Charles R. McCormick. We hauled lumber from the Pacific Northwest to the East Coast—through the Panama Canal. We came around one trip with 1,025,000 board feet on deck, besides the hold load. In one hold, we had wheat that we picked up in Stockton, California. That merchant fleet tour was from 1933 to 1936.

Again a civilian, Don worked back in the Athol area, including a tour in the Union Twist Drill shop where he was when World War II broke out. Expressing obvious distaste for the job, Don noted, "I was filing—and not pieces of paper in a drawer!

Filing. I didn't believe it. I'd look at the job and look out the window at the UTD canal and wonder what I was doing there. Then that Sunday, the Japs did it [the Japanese bombed the United States Naval fleet in Pearl Harbor, Hawaii, to begin

World War II.]

Monday, I was teetering down to Fitchburg with my little paper—the statement of service. In theory, one third would be in the Navy, one third in the reserves, and a third out drifting around on call. The recruiter said, "We wouldn't need you guys. In a couple of weeks, this will be all done." Back I went to UTD.

Finally, they instituted a manpower request. They needed everybody. In fact, they were asking for any pictures of Japan that anybody had. I got a letter from the Office of Man-power, a federal thing. It said something like, "It has been shown that you have had ten years' experience in a critical occupation." I could see myself in a merchant ship bound for Murmansk. I said to myself "I'm going to do that." I chop, chop, chopped down and shipped in to an outfit that was a small boat outfit. We wound up everywhere.

The outfit went to the South Pacific and everywhere else, but I didn't. In 1943, while in Argentia, Newfoundland, I started coughing all the time. I went to see "Doc." It scared the Bejeebers out of me when the doc said "You ever had TB—" and he didn't stop, "—before?"

I said, "Have I got it now?"

He said, "You're going back to the States."

World War II wasn't much for me. They shipped me to the Naval hospital in Chelsea, Massachusetts. After about a month, they shipped me to the VA [Veterans Administration] in Rutland. Then I was there forever, in Rutland. They finally did surgery on me, removing part of the lungs.

Glossary

SOURCES:

Famous Bombers of the Second World War by William Green. Hanover House, Garden City, New York. 1960. 136 pages.

Jane's Fighting Ships 1944-45. MacMillan Company, New York. 1947.

Jane's Fighting Ships of World War II. Military Press, New York, 1989. 320 pages.

Rand McNally Encyclopedia of Military Aircraft 1914-1980, edited by Enzo Angeluco. Rand McNally and Company, Chicago. 1981. 546 pages.

World's Fighting Planes by William Green and Gerald Pollinger. Hanover House, Garden City. New York. 1961.

GERMAN AIRCRAFT
ME 109 by Messerschmitt
Fighter first made in 1935, it was considered the best fighter in the world. Production was uninterrupted until 1945. Thirty-five thousand were produced. Early version had Junker Jumo 610 HP engine, but later versions had Daimler-Benz DB601 engine.

Hindenburg
Airship or dirigible (called a zeppelin) designed by Count Ferdinand von Zeppelin. Filled with hydrogen, it was the largest aircraft constructed. It went down 2 May 1937 in Lakehurst, New Jersey.

JU-88 by Junker
German fighter developed in 1941 and operational in 1943. It was used as a night fighter, intruder, and high-altitude reconnaissance aircraft. It was powered by a 1,700-HP BMW or a 1,600-HP Jumo engine.

JAPANESE AIRCRAFT
(as identified with United States GI nicknames)

Betty **Bomber G4M by Mitsubishi**
Large twin-engine bomber first made in 1937. In all, 2,446 were produced making it the most widely used Japanese bomber.

Judy **D4Y Suisei by Yokosuka**
Imperial Navy's carrier-based bomber, powered by a *V*12 liquid-cooled engine.

Tony **Ki-61 Hein by Kawasaki**
Single-seat fighter and fighter bomber. The *Tony* was the only Japanese fighter with a liquid-cooled engine, an 1,175-HP, 12-cylinder DB601A by Daimler-Benz.

Zero **A6M Zeke by Mitsubishi**
Single-seat Japanese fighter and fighter bomber. With its 1,130-HP engine, the *Zero* could reach top speeds of 356 MPH and a ceiling of 19,680 feet. A total of 10,499, the most of all Japanese planes, was produced between 1939 and 1945.

UNITED STATES AIRCRAFT

Manufacturers' Designations

United States Navy

A - Brewster Aeronautical
B - Boeing and/or Beech
C - Curtiss and Curtiss-Wright
D - Douglass
E - Bellanca
F - Grumman
G - Great Lakes
H - Hall-Aluminum or Stearman-Hammond
J - North American
K - Fairchild
L - Bell
M - Martin
N - Naval Aircraft Factory
O - Lockheed
P - Spartan
R - Maxson or Ryan
S - Vought-Sikorsky or Stearman
T - El Segundo plant, Douglass (was Northrop)
U - United or Vought
W - Waco
Y - Consolidated
X - experimental

Akron **by Goodyear**
Airship or dirigible. Destroyed in an accident in 1935. United States airships were inflated with the non-inflammable gas helium.

Los Angeles
German airship, or dirigible, captured in World War I and renamed.

A-36
Army version of the *Dauntless* by Douglass. In April of 1942, the *Mustang MKI*, an A-36, was put into service. The United States ordered five hundred of a version that had been adapted as a dive bomber—the A-36A.

AD-6 *Skyraider* **by Douglass**
Single-seat attack bomber powered by 2,700-HP Wright radial engine. Speed: 365 MPH at 15,000 feet with 10,000 pounds of ordnance load.

AT-6 *Texan* **by North American**
Trainer (advanced), first produced in 1940. Low wing, retractable gear. 600-HP constant-speed propeller.

BT-13 *Valiant* **by Vultee Aircraft Company**
Bomber and bomber trainer. First appeared in 1939. In all, 11,537 were built for the United States Navy and Army Air Corps. 450-HP engine with two-position propeller.

B-24 *Liberator* **by Consolidated**
1939 bomber with Pratt and Whitney turbosupercharged engines. A total of 18,188 were built—more than any other model. B-24s were credited with dropping 635,000 tons of bombs and shooting down 4,189 enemy planes.

B-25 *Mitchell* **by North American**
Bomber named after General Billy Mitchell. Equipped with two 1,350-HP engines (later versions had 1,700-HP Wright radial) and tricycle landing gear. Gained fame when Major General Jimmy Doolittle's raiders flew from the aircraft carrier USS *Hornet* to bomb Japan in 1942.

B-26 *Marauder* **by Martin**
Two 2,000-HP-engine bomber. Crew of five, including two gunners. Speed: 320 MPH and range greater than 1,500 miles.

B-29 *Superfortress* **by Boeing**
Big bomber with production first ordered in 1941; first flight: September, 1942. Speed: 365 MPH, altitude 30,000 feet, and bomb load of 10,000 pounds. B-29s dropped atomic bombs on Hiroshima and Nagasaki, Japan, to end World War II after doing extensive service throughout the Pacific Theatre.

C-47 Military version of the DC-3 by Douglass for United States Army Air Corps
Transport plane for troops and materiel. Some 13,000 1,200-HP-Pratt-and-Whitney-twin-engine plane were produced. The National Air and Space Museum calls it "...the single most important aircraft in the history of air transportation."

C-54 *Skytrain* **by Douglass**
Transport based on the DC-4. A four-1,530-HP-engine airplane that flew 200 MPH at 15,000 feet and had a ceiling of 26,600.

C-56 *Lodestar* **by Lockheed**
Twin-engine plane well known in 1940 as the *Model 18* airliner.

C-123 *Provider* **by Fairchild**
Assault transport with two 2,500-HP Pratt and Whitney engines. Cruise speed: 186 MPH. Maximum speed: 253 MPH and ceiling of 24,000 feet.

C-130 *Hercules* **by Lockheed**
Assault transport introduced in 1955, with four 3,750-HP Allison turboprops. Cruise speed: 335 MPH. Maximum speed: 380 MPH. Maximum weight, loaded: 124,200 pounds.

F4U *Corsair*
F4U-1 *Corsair Scout* **by Vought-Sikorsky**
Single seat, inverted gull-wing plane with a Pratt and Whitney 2,000-HP air-cooled engine.

P airplanes were built for pursuit.
P-38 *Lightning* **by Lockheed**
Two-seat long-range fighter and fighter/bomber with two 1,225 HP Allison 12-cylinder liquid-cooled engines. Speed: 360 MPH at 10,000 feet. Maximum speed: 395 MPH. Ceiling 39,000 feet.

UNITED STATES AIRCRAFT (continued)

P-39 *Airacobra* by Bell

Tactical support aircraft with tricycle landing gear. Of the 9,558 produced, the Union of Soviet Socialist Republics received 4,773. Speed: 400 MPH at 15,000 feet. Ceiling: 30,000.

P-40 *Tomahawk* by Curtiss

Fighter/bomber P-40E was called the *Kittyhawk* and the P-40 F through M were called the *Warhawk*. It was powered by a 12-cylinder, 1,150-HP Allison liquid-cooled engine. Speed: 352 at 15,000 feet. Ceiling: 32,400.

P-47 *Thunderbolt* by Republic

Fighter/bomber powered by a 2,300-HP Pratt and Whitney radial air-cooled engine. Speed: 428 MPH. Able to fight as high as 35,000 feet.

P-51 *Mustang* by North American

Single-seat, single-engine land-based fighter with three machine guns in each wing. 1,490-HP Packard engine built by Rolls-Royce. Speed: 437 MPH and "unequaled" range.

PBY *Catalina* by Consolidated

Patrol bomber capable of takeoff and landing on land or water. Prototype flew in 1935, but the first amphibious version (PBY-5A) flew in 1941.

Piper *Cub*

Built for observation, general aviation, and used as a trainer. Called the *Grasshopper* by the United States Army Air Corps, which ordered it in 1941. Several versions were made.

PT-17 *Kaydet* by Stearman

Biplane primary trainer with tandem seats with 7-cylinder radial air-cooled Continental engine capable of 220 HP.

SBD-2C *Helldiver* by Curtiss

Attack bomber with one 1,900-HP Wright radial engine. Maximum speed: 294 MPH at 16,700 feet.

SBD-4 *Dauntless* by Douglass

Dive bomber and mainstay of United States Navy and Marine aviation at the beginning of the Pacific war. One 1,200 HP radial engine.

T-28 *Trojan* by North American

First military trainer with a tricycle undercarriage. Powered by one 1,425-HP Wright Cyclone radial engine. Speed: 346. Cruise speed: 250. Ceiling: 37,000 feet.

UNITED STATES NAVY AND COAST GUARD SHIPS

Tonnage is based on displacement of water. Beam equals width measured at widest point of hull.

Balao class submarines were 311.75 feet long with a 27-foot beam and equipped with ten torpedo tubes. Gato class submarines had a similar silhouette.

Baltimore class ships were heavy cruisers built in 1940.

Shipbuilding companies frequently had the initials *S.B.* or *D.D.* in their company names. *S.B.* means *ship builder*. *D.D.* means *dry dock*.

Discrepancies in ship specifications are sometimes found from reference source to reference source.

The following explanation of ship names is from ***Jane's Fighting Ships Of World War II.***

Battleships are named after States; heavy and light cruisers after large cities; aircraft carriers after historical naval vessels or battles; destroyers after officers and enlisted men of the Navy and Marine Corps, Secretaries of the Navy, Members of Congress, and inventors.

Submarines are named after fish and marine creatures; minesweepers and submarine rescue vessels after birds; gunboats and escort vessels after small cities; submarine tenders after pioneers in submarine development and mythological characters; repair ships after mythological characters; oilers after rivers; store and cargo ships after stars; destroyer tenders after natural areas of the United States, e.g., mountain ranges, valleys, etc.; large seaplane tenders and aircraft escort vessels after sounds; ammunition ships after volcanoes and ingredients of explosives; transports after flag officers, general officers, and officers of the Marine Corps; attack transports and attack cargo ships after counties; coastal minesweepers after abstract qualities, etc.; small seaplane tenders after bays, straits, and inlets; ocean-going tugs after Indian tribes; and harbor tugs after Indian chiefs and words of the Indian dialect.

Owing to war exigencies, occasional exceptions to this system will be found.

LCI
Landing Craft Infantry
387 tons, 159 feet long, 23 2/3-foot beam, 1,320 HP. Speed: 14 knots.

LCP
Landing Craft Personnel

LCS(L)
Landing Craft Support (Large)

LCT
Landing Craft Transport
285 tons, 114 1/2 feet long, 32 2/3-foot beam, 675 HP. Speed: 10 knots.

LCVP
Landing Craft Vehicle Personnel

LSSL
Landing Ship Support Large

LST
Landing Ship Tank
4,080 tons, 328 feet long, 50-foot beam, 1,700 HP. Speed: 11 knots.

PC-45
130-foot Coast Guard patrol craft.

UNITED STATES NAVY AND COAST GUARD SHIPS (continued)

USCGC Tampa
Cutter built 1921 by General Engineering and Dry Dock Company of Oakland, California. 1,780 tons. 24 feet long. 39-foot beam.

USS Arizona (BB-39)
Battleship. Built 1915. 32,600 tons. Torpedoed and bombed on by Japanese in Pearl Harbor, Hawaii, on 7 December 1941.

USS Barbel
Submarine. Built 1943. 1,526 tons. Reported missing in Borneo waters February 1945.

USS Blueback
Balao class submarine. Launched May 1944 by Electric Boat, New London, Connecticut.

USS Bush.
Destroyer. Completed February, 1919, by Fore River.

USS Chilton (APA)
Amphibious assault ship.

USS Constitution
Frigate first commissioned in 1794. 199 feet long. 34-foot beam. Called "Old Ironsides." Crew: two officers and ten sailors.

USS Dobbin (AD-3)
Destroyer tender built at the Philadelphia Navy Yard and commissioned in 1924. 8,325 tons. 483.83 feet long. 61-foot beam. Used as a yacht by the Secretary of the Navy.

USS Halfbeak
Balao class submarine built by Electric Boat during the 1943-1944 program. Diesel powered. Top speed: 21 knots.

USS Hollandia
Light fleet aircraft carrier built in 1944. 6,730 tons. 498 feet long. 80-foot beam. Complement: 800.

USS Indianapolis (CA-35)
Heavy cruiser built by New York S.B. in Camden and commissioned in 1933. 9,950 tons. Torpedoed by a Japanese submarine northeast of Leyte 29 July 1945.

USS James, Reuben(DD-245)
Destroyer commissioned in 1920. 1,190 tons. Sunk by a German submarine on 31 October 1941 while escorting a convoy of lend-lease cargo bound for England.

USS Memphis
Light cruiser completed in 1925 by Wm. Cramp & Sons, Philadelphia. 7,050 tons. 555.5 feet long. 55.5-foot beam. Complement: 458.

USS Montcalm (AT-39)
Ocean-going Tug commissioned 1921. 1,050 tons. 149.25 feet long. 30-foot beam.

USS Nautilus (SS-168)
Diesel-powered submarine. 312 feet long. 27-foot beam. Operating depth to 300 feet.

USS New Mexico

USS Pomodon
One of 16 Corsair class submarines built at Portsmouth Navy Yard. 1,570 tons. Enlarged and improved version of the Balao design.

USS Poole (DE-151)
Destroyer escort built by Consolidated Steel Corporation. 1,200 tons. 306 feet long. 37-foot beam. Top speed: 21 knots. Complement: 220 men.

USS Quincy (CA-39)
Heavy Baltimore class cruiser by Bethlehem S.B. Co., Quincy, Massachusetts, commissioned in 1936. 9,375 tons. Torpedoed in action in 1942. A second ship (CA-71), the former USS Saint Paul was named the Quincy in 1943. 13,600 tons.

USS Randall
Attack transport. 12,450 tons. 455 feet long. 62-foot beam. 24 feet of displacement. 8,500-HP engine. Speed: 17 knots.

USS Relief
Hospital ship completed in 1919 by Philadelphia Navy Yard. 7,275 tons. 460 feet long. 61-foot beam.

USS Ringgold (DD-500)
Destroyer built by Federal S.B. & D.D. Co. One of 145 built during the "emergency program" of 1940 and launched in 1942. 2,050 tons. Top speed: 35 knots. Complement: between 250 and 300 men.

USS Saratoga
Aircraft carrier built in 1925. 33,000 tons. 888 feet long. 106-foot beam. Complement (including flyers) 169 officers and 1,730 men.

USS Scabbardfish
Balao class submarine built at Portsmouth Navy Yard and launched in 1944. One 3-inch .50-caliber gun and ten torpedo tubes.

USS Toro (SS-422)
Balao class submarine built at the Portsmouth Navy Yard and launched in 1944.

USS Tunny (SS—282)
Submarine built at Mare Island during the 1940 "emergency program." 1,525-tons. Six forward torpedo tubes and four aft tubes.

USS Utah (AG-16)
Battleship BB-31). Completed in 1911. 23,033 tons. 521 feet long. 88-foot beam. Complement: 944.

USS Whale (SS-239)
Gato class submarine built at Mare Island during the 1940 program and launched in 1942. 307 feet long. 27-foot beam.

Index